The Divided Soul

The Divided Soul

DUTY AND DESIRE
IN LITERATURE AND LIFE

Heidi White

GOLDBERRY PRESS
CONCORD, NC
2025

PUBLISHED BY GOLDBERRY PRESS,
AN IMPRINT OF GOLDBERRY BOOKS LLC
Copyright © 2025 Heidi White

ISBN: 979-8-9927698-0-7

Printed in the United States of America. First Edition.

All rights reserved. No part of this book may be reproduced, in any form, without written permission from the publisher, except for the purposes of review, in which case brief passages may be quoted alongside the appropriate credits. No part of this book may be stored in a retrieval system, or transmitted in any form or by any means—electronic, digital, mechanical, or otherwise—without written permission from the publisher. For promotional or review copies, including for institutional use, please write to info@goldberrybooks.com.

Cover design by Graeme Pitman.

Goldberry Press
12 Union Street South
Concord, NC 28025

1 2 3 4 5 6 7 8 9 0

For more information please visit goldberrypress.com.

*To my brave mother,
who taught me how to love.
May your memory be eternal.*

*To C.S. Lewis—Saint Jack,
"through you, I was a poet;
through you, a Christian."*

—PURGATORIO 22.73

*To Scott.
"I am my beloved's,
and his desire is for me."*

—SONG OF SONGS

"Do you not want the King?"

"Want him?" she said, "How could there be anything I did not want?"

—PERELANDRA

CONTENTS

Introduction / 1

CHAPTER ONE / 21
Splendid Sufferings: Duty in the Divided Soul

CHAPTER TWO / 41
Endless Distances: Desire in the Divided Soul

CHAPTER THREE / 59
The Greatest of These is Love: Love, Repentance, and Endurance

CHAPTER FOUR / 77
A Noble Telos: Marriage and Comedy

CHAPTER FIVE / 93
The Turning of the Wheel: Death and Tragedy

CHAPTER SIX / 111
The King and the Man: The Drama of Succession

CHAPTER SEVEN / 129
Elinor Dashwood in search of the Holy Grail: Desire Submerged in Duty

CHAPTER EIGHT / 145
Agents and Objects: Feminine Desire in Literature

CHAPTER NINE / 163
Formal Longing: Duty and Desire in Poetry

CHAPTER TEN / 179
Forms of Fidelity: Overcoming the Modern Tyranny of Desire

CHAPTER ELEVEN / 197
The True Myth: Restoring the Broken Images

CHAPTER TWELVE / 213
The Divine Physician: How Christ Heals the Divided Soul

INTRODUCTION

STORIES AS ICONS

How Literature Reflects the Divided Soul

My grandfather died when I was eight years old. I remember him as children do, in images and impressions—heavy jowls and white whiskers looming over me, an immense belly slung over belted slacks, a private office furnished with a vast, hand-hewn mahogany desk and a black leather office chair. I remember the resonance of his deep voice and the deeply-etched corners of his mouth. Mostly I remember the posture of cringing timidity that characterized my mother during our visits to my grandparents' home on the black crags of the Northern California coast. I accepted this as one of her many baffling incarnations. This one, at least, was predictable.

Their home was full of wondrous objects. Orange leather chairs. A backlit Robinson map in the hallway that cast an eerie blue light along the corridor at night. Knobbly water goblets made of green glass. Overgrown honeysuckle vines populated with wine-colored hummingbirds with iridescent green heads. Great glass buoys hanging over the wooden deck rails in webbed ropes, like captive tears. A vivid painting of the many-armed Hindu goddess, Kali, enthroned within a pink Lotus flower, her smile as mysterious as the Mona Lisa's. The house itself was a sprawling 1960s ranch-style home of weathered gray clapboard built into a cliff overlooking the dark and oily waters of the San Francisco Bay. Ice plant and pampas grass grew in the crags and rills, and eucalyptus trees filled the air with astringent spice. I wanted to love everything in that strange and curious house, and sometimes, if I was left alone, I did.

My grandfather died a lingering death from leukemia. Since I was his favorite grandchild, he called for me as he lay dying, and for hours I perched on a stool next to his portable hospital bed—I remember instruments beeping, cords dangling, insects buzzing, my legs swinging—in the basement of that gray house on the bay while he told me stories about himself. He was the seventh of thirteen children. He picked cotton as a boy in hand-me-down overalls. He killed a rattlesnake with his shovel. He taught himself to read and became a polymath and an autodidact. He won my grandmother's hand from the threat of another suitor. He led a battalion up the beach under fire in the invasion of the Philippines in World War II. He became a botanist and a professor at UC Berkeley. He piloted a sailboat to Guam, the West Indies, the British Virgin Islands. All these things I remember or think that I remember. I know now that I was chosen to be the keeper of his memories.

After he died, two essential things happened. The first is that he made my fragile mother the executor of his complex estate, a difficult role that catapulted her into the chaos and despair that haunted the remainder of her life. The second is that he bequeathed her his books. At first I did not recognize this second gift. As my mother spent more and more days in her bedroom with the blinds drawn, I nearly sank into my own kind of stupor by watching long hours of television. When she discovered this, she forbade it. I had to find something else to do. One day, bored and listless, I opened a book—*Anne of Green Gables*. I am sometimes filled with awe that such small movements of the body and the will—pulling a book randomly off a shelf, sliding my eyes over its cover, wetting my finger to turn a page, beginning to read—can produce such definitive transformations.

Anne of Green Gables saved my life. Right away I recognized that young Anne Shirley, red hair notwithstanding, was just like me—lonely, grieving, disoriented, unguarded, bewildered, stranded in a universe of insoluble contradictions. How can a world be simultaneously laden with such deprivation and beauty? But Anne clung to beauty while I was on the razor's edge. Avonlea's images, events, places, and people soon colonized my inner life. Unconsciously I imitated Anne. While my mother barricaded herself behind the locked bedroom door, I took walks, picked flowers, baked, wrote stories, sang as I worked, and named places and things that I loved. Behind the abundant white lilac bushes at the end of our cul-de-sac, I constructed a private haven such as Anne would glory in. There the sunlight filtered through the waxy leaves to the warm, bare dirt where I stashed a picnic blanket, tea cups, a shoebox of collected treasures (I remember a pearly snail shell and a crystal button), and a drawstring bag of books, including *The Secret Garden* and *Little Women*. I hid there to read, to imagine, to write in my journal, and to compose stories, poems, and reflections. In that lilac-scented refuge, I became a reader, a thinker, and a writer.

But the book was not done with me yet. As I read and reread *Anne of Green Gables*, something eternal began to grow in me. I gradually wanted to love what Anne loved and to reject what she rejected. Instead of gossiping and complaining, I learned to hold my tongue. Rather than sink into melancholy, I developed wholesome habits. I no longer envisioned God as a withholding taskmaster, but as the loving and generous Creator of the beauty and richness I now loved. *Anne of Green Gables* did not erase my confusion and sadness, but it built a scaffolding of holy desire in me. It gave me eyes to see. Anne awakened the deadened longings of my bereft childhood.

Such is the power of a story. Furthermore, such is the power of one story meeting and changing another. Before Anne, my life was becoming a prescribed narrative on a downward trajectory. The plot? Predictable. *Extra! Extra! Read all about it! Lonely, Anxious Little Girl Absorbs the Sins and Sufferings of the Previous Generations while Absolutely Nobody Pays Attention!* But this embryonic tragedy was averted by another story. Stories can do that. Much ink has been spilled by scholars and theologians about Jesus' habit of speaking in parables, but to me, it just makes sense. We become what we behold. We are the stories we tell ourselves.

Now that I am grown I am still defined by the stories that inhabit my mind and heart. So are you. Stories, far more than propositions, shape our interior geography. "A good myth, like a good map, enables the wanderer to survive, perhaps even to flourish, in the wilderness,"[1] wrote David Hicks. That was certainly true for that lost, little girl who found her way to goodness through *Anne of Green Gables*. But what makes stories so powerful? And what ought we to do about it? Those questions are the subject of this book.

Upon the wall above my desk hangs a collection of Christian icons depicting holy people, events, and theological truths. According to iconographers and devotees, icons are more than religious art. Rather, they are sacred artifacts, often described as windows into heaven, since they are believed to be visual representations of spiritual realities. They point beyond this world into a mysterious country that remains unknown and unexplored by the living. This raises the question: Are there artifacts equivalent to icons that incarnate more mundane and immediate realities?

I think that the answer to that question is yes—stories. Like icons, the world's great stories embody mystical and universal truths. Unlike icons, however, these truths are not always heavenly. They do not necessarily draw our attention to God, at least on the surface. Rather, they turn our eyes inward, into the nature of ourselves and this world. Stories are icons of human experience.

In these pages, we will explore all manner of iconic stories and the truths they convey. This is easier than it might seem because it turns out that the embedded patterns of universal reality found in stories are really quite simple. By "simple," I do not mean simplistic, but elegant, understandable, universal. As Socrates once argued nearly 2,500 years ago in the *Gorgias*, truth does indeed exist; it can be

---

1. Hicks, *Norms & Nobility: A Treatise on Education*, 29.

known, and—most importantly for the purposes of this book—it can be *told*.

I will propose in the following pages that all enduring and honest stories across history explore one fundamental enigma that traces back to the foundation of the world. This essential human mystery is not merely academic (although it can be studied academically) but primarily existential and thus lends itself to exploration through narrative rather than proposition. Interesting stories, after all, are not pedantic; they are far too risky and uncertain for that. Anything can happen in a story, but what is fascinating is that not anything *does*. Rather, the enduring stories of the world tend to distill down to universal preoccupations and premises. But why?

I think the world's great stories (including our own) dwell upon the mystery of one immense dilemma—the fallen nature of the world and our innate longing for its restoration. And what is the nature of this fallen reality? We learn it in the very first story of Adam and Eve, a familiar tale that reveals a great mystery: the primal division between duty and desire.

> *In the beginning, God created the heavens and the earth. The earth was formless and void, and darkness covered the surface of the deep. Into this nothingness and chaos, God spoke, "Let there be light," and His Word became light. God saw that it was good, and He kept on creating more and more goodness: the sun and the moon, the land and the sea, the plants and the animals, and finally—best of all—a Man, made from the earth itself, whose name was Adam,*

which means what he is: a man. God made the man in His own image, in the Image of God He created him, and He gave the man work that imitated His own work: to name the animals what they are and to tend the goodness He had made.

God gave the man a flourishing garden for his home. But the man was lonely, because he did not have a strong helper by his side in the great work God had given him. God caused the man to fall into a deep sleep, and while he slept, God took a rib from the man's body and fashioned it into a strong and beautiful companion. She was called Woman, for she was taken out of the man and made into herself.

And now there were two beings made in God's Image, in the Image of God who created them, male and female He created them. The man loved the woman, and brought her to the garden. They dwelled there, delighting in the whole world and in each other. All things were theirs and nothing was not, except for one tree, which bore a dangerous fruit of the knowledge of good and evil. God told them not to eat the fruit, for it would corrupt them unto death, and then they would no longer have God, the whole world, and each other to delight their hearts. The man and woman understood, and for a time all was good.

But soon a great evil invaded the sacred garden: a cunning monster, more cunning than the other beasts, whose dark heart was riddled with pride and envy. He knew good and evil, and he hated the good.

One day, the woman lingered near the forbidden tree, and the monster spoke to her. "Did God really say you cannot eat from any tree in the garden?"

Surprised, the woman corrected the monster. "We can eat the fruit from any tree we desire—all of them, except one," she gestured to the forbidden tree, "This one. We shall not even touch it, lest we die."

"You shall not die," hissed the monster, "But you shall become wise, like gods, knowing good and evil."

The woman gazed at the fruit, and saw that it was beautiful, and good to eat, and desirable to make her wise. She plucked it and ate it. She gave some to her husband, who was with her, and he ate it. As soon as it touched their lips, they were changed. They looked down at their bodies, and for the first time they knew that they were naked. Fleeing, they cloaked their nakedness with leaves.

Later, in the cool of the day, God came to dwell with them, but He could not find them. He called for them, and they came trembling, covered in leaves. "Where are you?" God called to the man.

"I heard you calling to me, but I was ashamed, because I was naked, so I hid." God's face was stern. "Who told you you were naked? Have you eaten from the tree whereof I commanded you not to eat?"

And then the man showed once and for all that he had changed. He pointed his finger at the woman, the beloved of his heart, and accused her.

"The woman you gave me, she gave me the fruit, and I ate it."

God turned His stern face to the woman. "What have you done?"

Trembling, the woman pointed to the monster. "The serpent beguiled me," she said, pointing her finger, "And I ate."

Now God's stern face looked at the monster.

"Because you have done this," God said to him, "You are cursed above any beast of the earth. On your belly you shall crawl, and you shall eat dust all the days of your life. And I will put enmity between you and the woman, between your seed and hers, and he shall crush your head, and you shall bruise his heel."

To the woman, God said, "I shall greatly multiply your pain in childbearing. In sorrow shall you give birth to children. Your desire shall be for your husband, and he will rule over you."

To the man, God said, "Because you have done this and listened to the voice of your wife, cursed is the ground because of you; in sorrow shall you eat of it all the days of your life.

Thorns and thistles shall it bring forth to you, and you shall eat of the grass of the field. By the sweat of your brow will you eat, until you return to the ground, for out of it were you taken; for dust you are, and unto dust will you return." Finally, God said, "Behold, the man has become like us, knowing good and evil. If he stays in the garden, he will eat from the tree of life and live forever, corrupted unto death." So God in his severe mercy sent the man and the woman away from the garden, and he placed Cherubim with a flaming sword to guard the entrance to the tree of life.[2]

This familiar tale is the very first story, and it is an icon of the nature of the world. From this story we learn that everything was created wholly good and wholly beloved by its Creator, but also vulnerable because of one essential aspect of the human soul—the capacity to choose. Free will remains the colossal risk of creation and of every story from then till now. We do not know how long Adam and Eve dwelled in Paradise, only that Paradise did not last forever, because there came a time when the man and woman chose to claim the sole forbidden thing.

But in a garden created for delight, how did the invading monster tempt Eve to ingest the fruit? The story records that he was more cunning than the other beasts. Through subtle and clever innuendo, he persuaded the woman that God's mandate to avoid the Tree was a deceptive obstacle to her happiness. He convinced her that her duty to obey her creator was a threat to the fulfillment of her desires.

And now we have arrived at the crux of the mystery that

---

2. Paraphrased and retold from Genesis 1-3 (KJV).

every story from Eden onward lays bare: the primal division between duty and desire. Before Eve sank her teeth into the fruit, there was no such division. Her duties and her desires were wholly unified. God made a fruitful garden of delights for the eye and the belly; He gave them righteous dominion and meaningful work. He gave them one another, each a counterpart to the other's glory. He withheld nothing that was good. Rather, he blessed their union, their authority, their bodies, and their appetites. Even the command to eschew the Tree of Knowledge of Good and Evil was neither arbitrary nor difficult in light of the abundance of goodness that surrounded them. Most theologians across Christian history have even agreed that the command was always temporary and that God intended to grant access to the fruits of the tree at the proper time. Until then, they were told to refrain. The duty to abstain existed only to protect the gratification of desire.

In Eden, Adam and Eve gratified their bodies and souls without sin. In fact, not only were they *allowed* to fulfill their appetites, they were *commanded* to do so. God told them to eat, reproduce, tend, name, and rule, all within a flourishing and sumptuous garden. At first these pleasures were not temptations, but joyful responsibilities for sinless souls. Their duties and their desires were altogether unified.

The fall of Adam and Eve is the saddest story in the history of the world because when Eve bit into the fruit, the link between duty and desire was severed. This rupture remains so traumatic that we are all still reeling, and out of our reeling, we tell the story of the fall over and over again.

The world's enduring stories, with their universal patterns and preoccupations, are the collected iconography of corrupted creation.

In C.S. Lewis's novel, *Perelandra*, an English professor named Dr. Ransom is sent to a sinless planet to prevent the fall of its two inhabitants. On Perelandra, he meets a Green Lady who is majestic and beautiful—an unfallen Woman, powerful and innocent. Her husband, the King, is away on a journey. Curious about her apparent indifference to her husband's absence, Ransom asks the Green Lady, "But are you happy without the King? Do you not *want* the King?"

"Want him?" she replied, "How can there be anything that I did not want?"[3]

The question stuns me, which is all wrong. *Perelandra* presents an imaginative icon of a world without sin, where desire is holy and where there is nothing that its inhabitants do not want. If the Christian account of creation is true, it ought (and *ought* is the word of duty) to be inconceivable to live in a world we do not want. Instead we live in a world where *want* and *ought* have been divided. Thus, "What ought I do?" versus "what do I want to do?" becomes the fundamental question of human will, and the variations on the theme are infinite. Throughout our lives, we grapple with the tension between duty and desire. But how do we make sense of such a senseless separation? I think storytelling—fact and fiction—is our way of trying.

The division between duty and desire is ground zero of human suffering and depravity. Every day we are at war with

---

3. Lewis, *Perelandra*, 60.

ourselves. Since we continue to bite into forbidden fruits, our attempts to heal our broken souls are oriented to that primary and underlying division. And that's where stories are deeply important. As icons of the fallen world, stories haunt the chasm between duty and desire. At its most fundamental, literature is about characters who make choices out of their free will, and these choices always reflect the tension between *ought* and *want*. The first example is Eve, but she is only the first. The duty/desire dichotomy is embedded within every narrative.

This book proposes that every real-life person and every fictional character is fractured along the fault line of duty and desire. This is what I am calling *the divided soul*, which manifests in psychological, social, and spiritual contexts. The people we encounter, the art we create, the stories we tell, the societies we construct, and the cosmos we inhabit all carry within themselves recognizable and interpretable fractals of this division. In these pages we will look at many examples. Each chapter ponders a unique aspect of the divided soul in literature and life. No chapter is comprehensive. Think of this book as a guided tour through a great cathedral. Everything in a cathedral is designed to draw the soul to God, from door jambs to flying buttresses. The grandeur is too much to take in all at once. Imagine me, as the author of this book, giving you a tour of a cathedral I have long inhabited, drawing attention to essential defining features but passing by something purposeful and lovely that will reveal itself when you return. I wish we could linger to gaze at each meaningful detail, but it is too much to take in at once. No doubt you will notice omissions or nuances you wish I had included. When that happens, I will have done my job—you will no longer be a tourist, but an inhabitant of the cathedral yourself, with eyes to see more than I have shown you and thoughts to ponder in your own mind.

On the other hand, you also might think I say too much. In order to properly consider the divided soul in specific stories, I provide plot and character information—and sometimes that includes spoilers. I have tried to limit such revelations as much as possible in hopes that you will turn (or return) to the stories to fill in the gaps. I have also done my best to choose stories that I think will stand up just fine to spoilers, as the best books always do. Great books reward rereading, yielding up their treasures even if you already know what comes next. I ask your forgiveness if my thoughts intrude on your reading pleasures, and I hope that these reflections will spark fruitful encounters with the books and with your own divided soul.

But what do I mean by the terms *duty* and *desire*? When I say duty, I mean the standard by which we measure ourselves. Whatever fills in the blank after "I should . . ." is what we consider to be a duty. On the other hand, desire is a perceived fulfillment of an appetite or longing. It fills in the blank after "I want..." Both duty and desire are intrinsically good, but we distort them. As Christians, we understand that true duty and true desire are absolute. Our true duty is to keep Christ's commandments, and our true desire is to unite with Him in an eternal paradise. That never changes. However, much of the time we fail to connect duty and desire to their proper objects, consciously or unconsciously adhering to fallen distortions rather than eternal realities.

In this book we will explore fallen duty and desire in many degraded incarnations, but ultimately true duty and desire are incorruptible. Like everything about our fallen world, they will be reconciled within ourselves, our societies, and our cosmos.

Until then, we keep living and telling stories. But how does the divided soul manifest in the stories we live and tell? Turning first to duty, narratives explore duty in myriad contexts using different paradigms and models for "oughtness." The perceived duty of a warrior in, say, Homer's Greece is different from that of an impoverished maiden of marriageable age in Jane Austen's England, but the underlying tension between duty and desire remains the same. Sometimes characters avoid their duties, and sometimes they do not know which way duty lies. Savvy readers learn to identify the conflicts and standards by which characters in stories navigate the complexities of duty in a fallen world. In this book I will show you how to identify the manifold conflicted relationships to duty within characters and narratives in hopes of extending that understanding to our own divided souls.

Desire is perhaps more recognizable, identified in its fallen forms by those most identifiable and enduring categories: the lust of the flesh, the lust of the eyes, and the boastful pride of life. The pursuit of disordered desires is the subject of a plethora of tales. Sometimes, too, characters desire what is good—love, home, justice, forgiveness—but some obstacle or other prevents the fulfillment of their desires. We will look at many examples of these and other nuances of desire in stories and in ourselves.

Further complicating the issue is that duty and desire do not merely compete against each other, but duty often rages against duty and desire against desire. One example is found in Aeschylus' tragedy, *The Oresteia*. Noble Orestes is caught between two absolute but irreconcilable duties: one to avenge his father's murder by slaying the murderer and one to honor and protect his mother, who is the murderer. How is he to choose? The tension between competing duties creates the tragic action of the play. On the other side of the coin is the eponymous Anna Karenina from Leo Tolstoy's masterpiece. Anna is deeply attached to her son, her community, and her pampered existence in the upper echelons of the Russian aristocracy, but she also wants to build a life with her eager, dashing, younger lover. How is she to reconcile these contending desires? And what is she to do about her stagnant marriage and the rigid conventions of Russian society? These tangled threads of opposing *oughts* and *wants* generate the novel's poignant drama. When the various weaving and unraveling of strands like these unite in narrative form, we have a story—an icon of the fallen world.

But there is more. Since I am positing that all literature is, at heart, about the divided soul, the endeavor of this book is ambitious and immense. Perhaps it is worthwhile for the reader to inquire—what good will it do? Is this another abstract literary interpretation theory, suitable only for scholars and specialists? I think not—at least, not to me. Rather, I agree with Aristotle that art imitates life; therefore, for those with eyes to see, art reflects life back to us in all its manifold shadows and brilliances. Through stories, we come to know ourselves, our neighbors, our cultures, and our cosmos. Thus, I am not really writing in a literary mode but an existential one. I am asking the following question: how can stories, as icons of the fallen world, teach us how to acknowledge, to endure, and perhaps even to heal the divided soul? Such a question makes this project even more ambitious and immense but also, I think, more necessary.

Ancient thinkers considered every person to be a little world–a microcosm of the universe embodied in the individual. Among other things, this means that the stories of our lives share a common narrative. We are all created good, we all fall into sin and suffering, and we all are rescued and restored by intervening grace. By extension, every tale in the literary tradition and every person who has lived on this earth reflects this universal story. Over the centuries, literature tells this tale in myriad ways, creating overlapping layers of meaning with fiction, psychology, and faith. This book dwells in that overlapping space. And underneath all of this is something else, something less tangible but more transcendent—my own urgent yearning for the healing of my divided soul. To that end, I will tell some of my own stories in these pages. That will not be easy for me. I am neither by nature nor by inclination a self-revelatory person. I am more like the wicked and lazy servant in Christ's parable who buries his talent in a field because he is afraid. But I have been given a life that is not my own; it was bought with a price, and I will pry my fingers off of it and offer it to you. Perhaps something in these inadequate musings will awaken that eternal longing in you.

I wrote this book because that eternal longing is universal and purposeful. The divided soul is only our temporary and fallen selves, but our permanent, heavenly selves will be reunited. We will be at one with ourselves and our world. In the kingdom of God duty and desire are not enemies, but friends. Imagine a world uncorrupted by evil, where everything we want is intrinsically *good*, and everything good is desirable. That is paradise, and attaining it is the culmination of the Christian life. "You make known to me the path of life; in your presence there is fullness of joy; at your right hand are pleasures forevermore."[4]

To that end, Christ became flesh and dwelled among us, restoring the unity of the fractured life of the world. Christ's life, death, and resurrection heals the wounds of the divided soul, which means that if we want to be whole, we must look to Him. For that reason this book assumes a way of seeing all stories in literature and life through a kind of spiritual vision. Although usually an advocate for reading books on their own terms, this particular examination of the division and restoration of duty and desire serves another endeavor entirely. My project here is to identify this universal pattern woven into the fabric of reality, discoverable everywhere in literature and life, and through this work to illuminate the glory of God.

Jewish culture has a saying that expresses the hopeful expectancy that all will be made right someday, even in a world fraught with dangers and temptations—"Next year in Jerusalem." That is how I feel about the aching division

---

4. Ps. 16:11 (NASB).

between duty and desire. Next year in Jerusalem, our duties will not feel like drudgery, but delight. Next year in Jerusalem, there will be nothing that we do not want. Next year in Jerusalem, we will behold not merely the icons, but the mysterious realities beyond them.

I

SPLENDID SUFFERINGS

Duty in the Divided Soul

"It is fitting that we should celebrate and be glad"
—Luke 15:32

If you wonder about my qualifications for writing this book, they are simple—my lifetime of experience as a divided soul. Every day in one way or another what I want to do collides with what I *ought* to do, causing more than a small amount of angst. More often than not the stakes are relatively low (does it really matter whether I have a green smoothie or a donut for breakfast today?), but occasionally the claims of duty compete with more insidious appetites—vainglory, lust, sloth, resentments. By now I am decades into the project of ruling myself, and perhaps I have somewhat gotten the hang of it, but that has not always been true. Take, for instance, my first day of kindergarten. I was to ride the school bus home, and anticipation burned within. When the bell rang I jetted to the bus laine. Mounting the top step, I was enthralled. *Here was Paul from my class! I liked Paul! This was living!* The ride was so exhilarating that when it screeched to a halt at my stop and I spotted my mother searching for me, I chose to stay where

I was. After all, I was on a magnificent adventure. At the next exit, Paul dismounted, and it occurred to me that my life as a Kindergarten wanderer might not end well. But there was still a boisterous crowd, so I made the best of it, meeting several new friends who exited the bus one by one until I was all alone. As the bus emptied, the panic rose. By the time the door closed behind the final commuter, I was crouched behind the last seat in the back row. When the bus driver called to me in a tired voice to come out from behind the seat and tell him where I lived, I burst into frightened wails. I was still sobbing when he pulled into the school parking lot where my long-suffering mother was waiting. This incident remains not only a vivid memory, but an ongoing metaphor for my prodigal life.

I told this story to a friend and received a blank stare. How could I have abandoned the secure plan to return home? Why did I gamble my mother's trust and approval? Didn't I think about getting in trouble? And why did I do it anyway? Just for fun?

"Yes," I told her. "Exactly. Didn't you ever do anything reckless just for fun?"

She shook her head.

"Never," she replied. "Even as a child, I always did the right thing. But I didn't have a lot of fun."

My friend's comment articulates the conflicted relationship we often have with claims of duty. Duty establishes our lives on secure foundations, providing boundaries to protect what we love and principles to guide what we do. Ever attentive to the right way, duty leads us to be steadfast, moderate, loyal, tenacious, and honorable. But duty divorced from desire is a demanding master, dictating rigid codes that often cause us to vacillate between poles of pride and shame in response to our own efforts and judgments. Like Atlas in the ancient myth, we shoulder the burdens of the world, but such unrelenting pressure erodes our capacity for delight. When duty alone rules the soul, joy is as fragile and ethereal as a spider's web.

Long ago I began mulling over duty's dilemmas after my godfather made a comment about the parable of the prodigal son. We were discussing something else entirely (which I have forgotten) when he caught my attention by remarking in an off-hand tone that "everything in life comes down to the story of the prodigal son." Something about his statement banged a gong, and I began to reflect on the allegory of duty and desire embedded within the parable.

> *Once there was a father who had two sons. The younger son demanded his share of the inheritance, which he squandered on wild living far from home. Soon the money was gone. Poverty-stricken, he hired himself out to feed pigs, and he was so hungry that he longed to feed himself with the slop.*
>
> *When he came to himself, he resolved to return to home and to say, "Father, I have sinned against heaven and against you. I am no longer worthy to be called your son. Make me like one of your hired servants." When he was still very far off, his father saw him and ran out to meet him. The boy said, "Father, I have sinned against heaven and against you. I am no longer worthy to be called your son," but his father interrupted him, calling out to his servants to kill the fatted*

calf and prepare a great feast to celebrate his return.

Meanwhile, the older brother, who had been working in the fields, heard music and dancing and asked a servant what it meant. "Your brother has come home," the servant replied, "and your father has killed the fatted calf for him." The older brother grew angry and refused to go in, so his father came out to plead with him. But he answered his father, "All these years I have worked for you and never disobeyed your commands, yet you have never even given me as much as a young goat to celebrate with my friends. But when this son of yours who has spent your money on prostitutes comes home, you kill the fatted calf for him!"

Son," he said, "you are always with me, and all I have is yours. But it is fitting that we should celebrate and be glad, for this brother of yours was dead and is alive again, was lost but now is found."[1]

Clearly the Father represents God, who demonstrates mercy to us as wayward sons, and the two boys can be understood as the two impulses of the divided soul. The Prodigal represents the desires that tempt us to squander God's good gifts on fleeting pleasures, leaving us famished and feeding on slop, a detail that cuts deeper when we remember Jesus told this story to a Jewish audience who considered pigs obscene. Also, ancient inheritance rights passed only through death, which means the Prodigal's underlying message to his Father is *I wish you were dead.* The

---

1. Paraphrased and adapted from Luke 15: 11-32 (KJV).

parable illuminates the potential for degradation that stalks human desire—a recognizable reality for anybody who has felt the lure of fleshly and worldly pleasures.

And what of the Older Brother? We know nothing about him until the Prodigal returns, when we discover that this whole time he has been laboring in the fields. When he realizes the Father is welcoming his rebellious brother home with a feast, he is angry and refuses even to come into the house, let alone attend a celebration. When his Father pleads with him to reconcile with his brother, the Older Brother lashes out at his Father, reminding him of his brother's crimes and accusing him of withholding the reward he believes he deserves for his faithful service. This pattern of relentless toil, thwarted hopes, and agonized recriminations marks the fractured psyche of the Older Brother, who represents duty divorced from desire. Dutiful souls suffer deeply when they reject desire, because desire whets our appetite for joy. Without desire, duty is mere drudgery. Older Brothers have many reasons to stifle desire—fear, disdain, scrupulosity, trauma, and more—but however valid these reasons may feel, over time they armor us against happiness. Duty was never meant to stand alone, but to reunite with the latent desires of the heart. Duty and desire are begotten by the same Father who grieves at their separation and invites them to reconcile.

I used to interpret the two brothers as categories representing types of people—some people are duty-driven Older Brothers and others are desire-driven Prodigals, and I still think that most of us, by our own unique combinations of nature and nurture, naturally tend towards the propensities of one over the other. But over time I have come to understand the brothers as representing innate impulses or tendencies within our interior lives—fragmented fallout from the original traumatic rupture in the garden of Eden. Within us dwell these two competing forces that grapple for dominance. But duty and desire were never meant to be enemies. They are brothers, and the Father longs for them to be reconciled. I have a dutiful Older Brother and a desiring Prodigal in me, and there is something especially poignant about the sins and sufferings of the Older Brother. What is it that motivates him to toil so tirelessly for his father? What does he actually want? And what will it take for him to recognize his father's love and reconcile with his brother?

Many stories explore variations on the theme of the Older Brother. One of the most iconic is the story of the mighty Trojan warrior, Aeneas, from Virgil's great Roman epic, the *Aeneid*. In both the epic and the parable, a dutiful son must decide whether or not to obey a divine father, but the results are opposite. If the Older Brother obeys, he will heal his divided soul, but Aeneas' obedience will doom him to remain divided.

The *Aeneid* has an interesting history. A few decades before the birth of Christ, Caesar Augustus commissioned Virgil to produce a national epic to celebrate the glory of Rome. The *Aeneid* extols Roman virtues—stoicism, endurance, dignity, and honor. In the fifth century AD, St. Augustine, unimpressed by the Roman spirit, scoffed at what was dubbed the "Splendid Vices" and urged Christians to avoid the pride and vainglory of the spirit of his age. He was right. The Splendid Vices may appear like virtues, but they exacerbate the divided soul because they divorce duty from desire, elevating stoic endurance above a humble and earnest desire for joy.

The epic's hero is Aeneas, a mighty Trojan demi-god who fought in the Trojan War. Aeneas' father is the mortal hero, Anchises, and his mother is Aphrodite, the goddess of erotic desire. Yet Aeneas is not like his mother. Duty is his destiny. Virgil conveys the essence of his hero in the epic's opening line: "Of arms and the man I sing, an exile driven on by fate."[2] Of arms—war. Of the man—Aeneas, an exile driven on by fate. And thus we learn everything we need to know about Aeneas, a warrior whose life is characterized not by his own choices, but by a conflict not of his own making and a fate not of his own will.

Aeneas' beloved city collapses in flames after the invading Greeks pull off the famous Trojan horse deception, and as the city burns, Aeneas runs into the fray, determined to die in glory. Primed for a heroic death, his battle frenzy is suddenly interrupted by the appearance of a ghost: the fallen Trojan prince Hector, who orders Aeneas to stop fighting and embrace another fate.

> *Escape, son of the goddess, tear yourself from the flames!*
> *The enemy destroys our walls, Troy is toppling from her heights.*
> *You have paid your debt to our king and native land.*
> *If one strong arm could have saved Troy, my arm*
> *Would have saved the city. Now, into your hands*
> *She entrusts her holy things, her household gods.*

---

2. Virgil, The *Aeneid*, 1.1.

> Take them with you as comrades in your fortunes.
> Seek a city for them, once you have roved the seas.
> Erect great walls at last to house the gods of Troy.[3]

Rather than die a glorious death, Aeneas' fate is to transfer the city's sacred objects and its displaced refugees to Italy where he will found a new city—Rome. True to his nature, Aeneas obeys, rushing into the burning streets with his beloved wife Creusa at his side. But in the chaos, Creusa falls.

> O dear god! My wife, Creusa—
> Torn from me by a brutal fate! What then,
> Did she stop in her tracks or lose her way?
> Or exhausted, sink down to rest? Who knows?
> I never set eyes on her again.[4]

Soon her ghost appears with a message from the gods.

> My dear husband, why so eager to give yourself
> To such mad flights of grief? It's not without
> The will of the gods these things have come to pass.
> But the gods forbid you to take Creusa with you,
> Bound from Troy together. The king of lofty Olympus
> Won't allow it. A long exile is your fate...
> There great joy and a kingdom
> Are yours to claim, and a queen to make your wife.
> Dispel your tears for Creusa whom you loved.[5]

---

3. Virgil, The *Aeneid*, 2.364-372.
4. Virgil, The *Aeneid*, 2.915-918.
5. Virgil, The *Aeneid*, 2.962-974.

Three times the weeping Aeneas attempts to embrace his wife, and three times his arms sweep through vapor. And then, in one of the most enduring images in literature, Aeneas carries his father on his back and leads his young son by the hand—three generations in one displaced, exiled figure—leaving his homeland forever, his face set toward his fate.

Creusa is the first sacrificial offering to the epic's Splendid Vices. Since the founding of Rome requires Aeneas to forge a political alliance with the native peoples through marriage, Creusa is in the way. She must die because it is his fate to marry an Italian princess and establish the new city. Creusa is sacrificed to the most Splendid Vice of all—Roman *pietas*. This quintessentially Latin term sounds like the English word "piety," but Christian piety is vastly different from Roman *pietas*. To us piety is almost exclusively sacred, but Roman *pietas* is an all-encompassing public duty—a laying down of one's personhood for the sake of civic good. Personal happiness is unimportant to Roman pietas. Only submission to duty matters. Aeneas is the ideal Roman hero, characterized wholly by *pietas*. Translators vary on how to convey *pietas* in English, often as "pious" or "devout," or—my personal favorite—"duty-bound." From the moment the ghost of Hector appears, Aeneas becomes a duty-bound agent of fate, forced from a life he loves, bereft of his wife, burdened by responsibilities, driven toward a conflict-ridden future.

Obedient to his fate, Aeneas and the Trojan refugees set sail for Italy, but along the way they stop for supplies on the shores of northern Africa, where he meets Dido, queen of Carthage. They become lovers, but their happiness is brief. Soon the gods intervene to recall Aeneas to his duty. He must cease his dalliance with Dido and continue on his way. He obeys. Dido, overcome with grief and rage, ignites her own funeral pyre, stabs herself, and dies wreathed in flames, cursing her lover.

Virgil uses the language of fire to describe Dido. She is perpetually "burning" with some passion—love, wrath, pity, sorrow. She represents the force opposed to *pietas*, which is *furor*. Often translated wrath, lust, or (of course) desire, furor is the enemy of *pietas*. As a result of constant *furor*, Dido commits follies, but other than a tendency to desire greatly, there is nothing intrinsically wrong with her that disqualifies her from marrying Aeneas. As befits a queen, she is gracious, courteous, regal, and accomplished. In fact, she does not even fall in love by her own will, but is pierced by Cupid's arrow during Aeneas' welcome feast. The mistakes she makes in the story are real but insufficient by modern sensibilities to warrant her destruction. But by Roman standards, Dido is the ravenous temptress of the epic. For one thing she is a rich and sensual African queen, and the Romans knew what that meant—Cleopatra, whom they loathed for enchanting not one, but two of their important statesmen and destabilizing the Roman political landscape. Secondly, Dido distracts Aeneas from his duty, threatening the fundamental Roman ethic of *pietas*. The fact that none of that is Dido's burden is immaterial to the epic, and within the ethical framework of the story, Dido deserves what she gets.

Dido is a product of the divided soul of her age. She represents the rejection of desire, and her fate demonstrates an inordinate elevation of duty. She suffers not for any grievous violation of desire, but simply for acting on desire at all. When Dido and Aeneas become lovers, Jove sends Mercury to redirect Aeneas from *furor* to *pietas*. Jove is alarmed because Aeneas wants Dido, and he sends his emissary to put a stop to it. Compelled by divine directive, Aeneas has no choice but to reject her and pursue his destiny. Consequently Dido immolates herself. On a symbolic level the point is obvious—embracing desire is an action of death.

Readers often have a visceral reaction to the rigid claims of duty in the *Aeneid*. I think that this is because we are not simply responding to Aeneas' burden, but to our own duty-bound lives. Who among us is not duty-bound? We are exiles from Eden, most of the time doing what we have to do rather than what we want to do. Our reactions to the epic reflect our inner posture toward lives of isolated duty. In my experience, duty-driven Older Brother types tend to have an attitude of grim acceptance toward Aeneas' fate. Troy is gone, Creusa is dead, Dido is a distraction, and the gods have decreed his future. He does what he has to do, they philosophize, and shrug their shoulders. Deep down such readers envision their own stoic adherence to a dutiful existence. On the other hand, desire-driven Prodigals often find Aeneas maddening, despising his decisions and interpreting him as flat, bland, hypocritical, or dishonest. Perhaps they are responding to their own fears that adhering to duty will lead to endless distress and deprivation.

However we interpret Aeneas, the Romans got something wrong that Christians get right. Duty will not always be divorced from desire. In the kingdom of God they will be united. The Romans cast *pietas* and *furor* as opposing forces, but Christians know that they were divided at the fall but will be restored, and along with their restoration will be the healing of the soul. Until then we live in tension. Our desires cannot be healed if we fail to fulfill our duties, nor can we enjoy our duty if we do awaken our proper desires. Ancient and medieval thinkers called desire eros after the young god shooting his piercing arrows into human hearts.

Somehow along the way Christians lost hold of *eros*, but pagan philosophy and Christian theology consider the healing wound of *eros* the proper ground-of-being for any meaningful goodness and happiness. The great Church Father, John Chrysostom wrote of Christ as "some ardent lover—or rather, more ardent than any lover."[6] He speaks of the pangs of eros, saying, "I am wounded with love for God."[7] He describes himself as painfully longing for union with God as a beloved longs to be united with a lover. He is not alone. Hundreds of Church fathers, theologians, scholastics, and mystics record the inconsolable yearnings of their hearts for the love of God. Of course this is also Biblical—the New Testament calls the Church the Bride of Christ, and many Old Testament references, such as Psalm 45, Hosea 11, and the entire book of Song of Songs, are allegories of eros between God and His people. Such language is ubiquitous in ancient and medieval Christianity, but largely lost in the post-Enlightenment West. For most of human history we have sought, not pushed away, the

---

6. Silouan Thompson, "Divine Eros According to Saint John Chrysostom."
7. ibid.

healing wound of love. The absence of eros in the Christian mind is a grievous loss to contemporary Christianity. Our divided souls are too prone to distrust and dismiss the desires of our hearts rather than welcome them as signposts to God.

This is probably because *eros* is painful. We do not know what to do with it. *Eros* rips us open, renders us vulnerable to sin, loss, and deprivation. The Greeks were on to something when they personified desire as a beautiful but dangerous youth armed with deadly bow and arrow. We fear desire, because it is so easily attached to improper and illicit objects. Most of us cannot help but equate desire with temptation. To protect our fragile hearts, we armor ourselves against the perils of desire with good works, as Aeneas and the Older Brother demonstrate. To Christians, eros is often a stranger and an enemy.

But Jesus never condemns desire in the parable. There is no quarter for Splendid Vices in the Christian faith; there is only the pursuit of joy. To that end, the Father prescribes the same remedy to each son—he invites them to the feast. A feast is more than a meal because it unites celebration with custom. Feasts offer an abundance of delicious and beautiful food governed by a system of convivial constraints about how to enjoy it. One dresses appropriately for a feast, sits at one's proper place, observes festal etiquette, and offers formal courtesies. Feasts unite duty and desire around a communal table.

The Father's goal for the feast is to heal the fractured Image of God in his sons. But it is the Prodigal, conditioned to desire, who accepts the invitation. His appetites are already fully alive, and his squalid ordeal among the pigs has made him ready to embrace the joy of a real feast. But the Older Brother is accustomed to deprivation. He already disdains his own appetites, so why would the return of an unworthy brother compel him to the table? He refuses to attend, bewildered and angry that he has labored without a reward for his worthiness. His brother's return awakens a painful longing he is unprepared to face, and he shuns him for it. In one thing he is right—the Prodigal must indeed repent of neglecting his duties, but the Older Brother must also repent of an error just as grave: disdaining his desires, which are awakened *on purpose* by the Father for their eternal fulfillment.

However, as every Older Brother knows, repentance is the rub. Dutiful souls are more comfortable proving their worth. The sins of the Older Brother, although more subtle, are as vicious as the Prodigal's: pride, envy, wrath, judgment, self-righteousness, vanity, accusation, hard-heartedness. They are not splendid at all, but debilitating. He is also suffering, as expressed in his haunted cry, "All these years I have worked for you and never disobeyed your commands, yet you have never even given me so much as a young goat to celebrate with my friends. But when this son of yours who has spent your money on prostitutes comes home, you kill the fatted calf for him!"[8] His words are a complaint, but they are also a plea. Underneath the dutiful exterior of the Older Brother lies a suppressed longing for love, for rest, for peace, for security, for delight. The Father's response cuts through his son's posturing to address his divided

---

8. Luke 15:29 (ESV).

soul. "Son, you are always with me, and all that is mine is yours." (Luke 15:31). With these words he blesses the efforts of his son's dutiful strivings. The Father is just as well as merciful, and he assures his son that he will not lose his reward for his faithfulness. Along with this consolation the Father has a final message. "But it is fitting that we should celebrate and be glad, for this brother of yours was dead and is alive again, was lost but now is found." (Luke 15:32). The Father solves the dilemmas of duty and desire with an invitation to come humbly to the feast.

Both Aeneas and the Older Brother are honorable sons, and the difference between the two is not so much in them, but in their fathers. Jove, called the Father of gods and men, requires Aeneas to meet the demands of *pietas* without regard for Aeneas himself. Yes, Jove will honor Aeneas with a glorious city and a royal bride, but Aeneas already has a city and a bride. Aeneas submits to the divine decree because he is honorable and obedient, not because he wants what the gods are offering. Like Aeneas, our dutiful souls are both strong and fragile—strong because we bear heavy burdens at great personal cost; fragile because we do not always know *why*. We often absorb the lie that desire is our enemy because the symbolic "fathers" in our lives impart duty-driven mandates. But the Father in the parable is entirely different. He demands no capitulation to implacable duty. Instead he comforts his anxious son and invites him to the feast.

Aeneas' experiences convey that dutiful endurance, however wholesome, is insufficient for human flourishing. We cannot white-knuckle our way to joy. We require an intervening mercy to offer help and hope. The duty-bound mission imposed by the gods and the deaths of Creusa and Dido are dark moments when we fear that the divided soul will remain broken forever. And our fears for Aeneas are justified. The epic does not end with a city and a bride after all, but with a fight to the death. When Aeneas arrives in Italy he finds a happy, thriving city on the verge of celebrating the wedding of Princess Lavinia to her suitor Turnus, the mighty warrior and prince of the neighboring Rutulian tribe. When Aeneas announces that he has come by will of the gods to marry Lavinia and establish a glorious city, Turnus is outraged. Burning with *furor* against his rival, Turnus' battle fury in the second half of the epic mimics Dido's erotic fury in the first half. War ensues, and Turnus is so driven by hatred that he slaughters Aeneas' young protege, Pallas, in cold blood. In response, Aeneas challenges Turnus to single combat—the winner gets Latium and Lavinia. Everybody knows that Aeneas is fated to found his city, but Turnus is so blinded by *furor* that he doesn't care. He fights savagely, but in the end Aeneas triumphs and Turnus is disarmed. Even in victory Aeneas is nearly persuaded to show mercy to his defeated foe until he sees that Turnus is wearing the sword-belt of the slain Pallas. Aeneas loved Pallas. He knows that Turnus wore the belt to taunt him, and for the first and only time in the epic, Aeneas gives way to *furor*.

> *Aeneas, as soon as his eyes drank in that plunder—keepsake*
> *Of his own savage grief, flaring up in fury*
> *Terrible in his rage he cries, "Decked in the spoils*
> *You stripped from the one I loved—escape my clutches? Never—*

Pallas strikes this blow, Pallas sacrifices you now,
Makes you pay the price with your own guilty blood!"
In the same breath, blazing with wrath (furor), he plants
His iron sword hilt-deep in his enemy's heart.[9]

The next lines are the final words of the epic.

Turnus turns limp in the chill of death,
His life-breath fled with a groan of outrage
Down to the shades below.[10]

What are we to make of this weighty action? Is this *furor* or *pietas*? Does it matter? Does it ennoble or degrade Aeneas? Is embracing furor supposed to heal Aeneas or further divide him? Textual evidence indicates that the epic remained unfinished—Virgil was notoriously obsessed with editing his own work—but I think the moral ambiguity of the closing scene is apt. Whether he was right to kill Turnus is uncertain, but it is clear that there is a natural man within the epic hero, and it is fitting that our last sight of duty-bound Aeneas is not his glorious destiny, but his divided soul. Aeneas ends the epic as he began it, an Older Brother laboring in the fields, waiting for a withholding father to remember to grant him a young goat.

But Jesus' parable offers a different vision for the dutiful soul. Here the Father accepts both of his sons with extravagant love. He runs to meet them both, first the Prodigal as he returns, and then the Older Brother when he refuses to

---

9. Virgil, The *Aeneid*, 12.1102-1110.
10. Virgil, The *Aeneid*, 12.1111-1113.

return. He wants one thing for both of his sons—to come to the feast. What makes the feast a healing occasion is that it is a good feast—a wholesome, satisfying, convivial celebration. Best of all, the Father is serving the fatted calf. Christian commentators interpret the fatted calf as an allegory of Christ and the Father's feast an allegory of the eucharist. Truly the feast is a healing communion in all senses of the word.

What we do not know, however, is whether or not the Older Brother ever comes. The parable ends with the Father exhorting his son to attend, but he never forces him. In this way too the Father is unlike the gods of this world, who exert their will through threat and compulsion. Not so the Father in the parable. He empowers his sons to choose for themselves. At the end of the story we do not know whether the Father's invitation accesses the buried *eros* that will lead the Older Brother to eternal joy. All of us encounter that same choice.

There is a Prodigal and an Older Brother in me. In my youth I was more prone to prodigal sins, as is no doubt apparent from the school bus escapade. But that, of course, is an example from my innocence, and there were other and darker instances of the same prodigal impulse. I know how that boy felt as he hungered for slop and longed for home. But now I am in my middle years, and my days are full of incessant duties. Since I am no longer very young, I know better than I once did about what is at stake if I were to neglect them, and so I press on. Sometimes I feel as though I am toiling in the fields with so much to do before the end of the day that if anybody were to invite me to a party, I would laugh in their face. I often need to reconnect with the desires of my heart. It seems good to me to be faithful and steadfast, but also to be happy—to order my will and my habits toward joy.

2

ENDLESS DISTANCES

Desire in the Divided Soul

"*Desire is full of endless distances.*"
—Robert Hass

I was well into adulthood when it dawned on me that I am not the hero of my own story. There were strong indications of this fundamental reality all along, but my powers of perception are weak. So little do I know myself that I mostly blame relationships or circumstances for my suffering. Looking back, this is ludicrous. Take my college years, for example. A few weeks into my freshman year, I met a boy and promptly fell dizzyingly in love. He had blue eyes and broad shoulders and a melancholy, intellectual soul, and I knew deep down in my desiring heart that this was the Real Thing. When he told me about the long-distance girlfriend he planned to marry, I dismissed the possibility out of hand. There was no way that a boy who read Hegel on Saturdays and looked into my eyes under the streetlamp amid the falling red leaves of October was going to marry another woman. The idea was preposterous. I knew that if I wanted and waited long enough, I would win my heart's desire. Years later I was bewildered when it finally broke through my thick haze of denial that the boy was indeed going to ruin my life by doing what he had said he would do all along. How could I have failed to win him over? What is this world that denied me what I wanted most?

Much later I faced another crisis of desire. My husband and I had a young son and a baby daughter. We hoped for more children, but I had a miscarriage. We mourned and tried again, only to lose another. Again and again it happened, loss after loss, hemorrhage after hemorrhage, over months and then years—seven times. My body could not hold onto my babies. One day, still pregnant with a baby I had learned that day had died in my womb, I sat on the stairs in the dark, grinding my knuckles into my eye sockets and shaking with sobs. Motherhood is *good*. I could not accept the magnitude of such senseless loss.

Some might have offered a platitude as I wept on the stairs. Be grateful for your many blessings, such a person would say. But I am a black hole. God forgive me, good things are never good enough. In this I do not believe I am alone. Humans are desiring creatures. We were created for fulfillment, and we grieve and rage when we cannot fully satisfy our longings. In this chapter we will wrestle with the problems and paradoxes of this Prodigal part of the soul.

Such a project is fraught. One of the problems in speaking of desire is that most of us feel ambivalent about it. Desire is dangerous. We have all suffered because of it, and it has often led us to commit follies and betrayals that we do not want to believe we are capable of—plus most of us feel that desire refuses to leave us well enough alone. But does desire only exist to plague us? Surely desire has a telos, an ultimate end for which it was created. When inquiring into the nature of something, the ancient philosophers taught us to ask three questions about it. *What is it? What does it do? What is it for?*

What is desire? It is an impulse to obtain completion that manifests in longing. What does desire do? Frankly, it hurts. Desire itself is not pleasurable, but painful, and we pursue its fulfillment as much to avoid its frustration as to satisfy its demands. Desire, wrote poet Robert Hass, "is full of endless distances,"[1] wounding us until we attend to it.

And what is desire for? That is easy. Desire exists to direct us toward delight. Without it, we have no capacity for happiness in this world or the next. In short, desire is our God-given prerequisite for joy.

Because desire is so powerful, it must be treated with care, and this is where the danger manifests. Wisely did C.S. Lewis write that our desires are not too strong, but too weak, that we are "fooling about with drink and sex and ambition when infinite joy is offered us, like an ignorant child who wants to go on making mud pies in a slum because he cannot understand what is meant by the offer of a holiday at the sea."[2] Sometimes this happens because we willfully choose to violate our duties, but more often we simply miss the mark, truly believing that these lesser things are what we want. We find ourselves disillusioned and disappointed, even enraged, and we double down or despair. In such cases the problem is not desire itself, but disordered desire—desire that lacks proper direction and

---

1. Hass, *Praise*, "Meditation at Lagunitas."
2. Lewis, *The Weight of Glory and Other Addresses*, 26.

attaches itself to elusive and insufficient objects.

Is there a ballast that counterbalances desire's often erratic impulses? Emphatically yes, and that ballast is duty. In the crucible of desire, laws and principles hold us steady, fortifying us to reject our baser appetites in favor of joy, which is desire's true object. We have already seen that obtaining joy requires an arduous pilgrimage fueled by love, repentance, and action. Joy is the *telos* of the harmonized soul where duty and desire unite as friends. Duty transforms desire from a tyrant to a guide, leading us to deny mud pies because we want a holiday at the sea. In short, if we want to be happy, we must learn to be good.

Literature is populated with desiring characters who wrestle in various ways with the claims of duty. Shakespeare's *Macbeth*, for instance, is a timeless cautionary tale against disordered desire. Macbeth fails to unite passion with principle, creating the conditions for his own tragic downfall. And he's not the only one—tragedies have followed a similar pattern for millennia. In *Poetics*, Aristotle proposed a literary criteria for tragedy, which he considered the highest form of narrative because it contains "an imitation of people who are better than we are."[3] According to Aristotle, characters are tragic because of actions they take *in excess* of their virtues. Since desire ought to be the seed of virtue, tragic characters meet tragic ends when they want to be happy but fail to be good.

Macbeth is a tragic character in this vein. At the beginning of the play, Macbeth is praised for his courage on the battlefield and his loyalty in the Scottish royal court.

---

3. Aristotle, *Poetics*, 53a.

Endless Distances

We meet him as he is returning from a military campaign during which he bravely quelled a rebellion against his cousin, good King Duncan. Riding home across the windswept Scottish landscape alongside his faithful comrade, Banquo, Macbeth seems to be a model of courtly virtue: he is brave, strategic, ardent, and patriotic.

But all is not as fair as it appears. Macbeth's journey across the "blasted heath"[4] is interrupted by three colluding witches, who greet him with, "Hail, Macbeth who will be king hereafter!"[5] With these tantalizing words, the witches arouse Macbeth's latent desire for the throne, swaying his fair virtues toward foul vices: "Fair is foul, and foul is fair,"[6] they declare ominously. His heroic virtues are real, not feigned—they spring from the desiring part of his soul whose instinct is to visualize a meaningful future and take action to create it, but his virtues become vices when he allows them to be corrupted by desire for power.

Literary opinion is divided on whether the witches' prophecy implanted Macbeth's ambition for the throne or merely exposed what was already there. Shakespeare embeds clues to Macbeth's moral deficiency from the start, like when he boasts of bribery to his wife. "I have bought golden opinions from all sorts of people."[7] Either way the essential point is clear—Macbeth is a man easily tyrannized by venal appetites. Soon his ambition manifests in treacherous brutality. By the final act, he has committed unimaginable atrocities, from murdering King Duncan in his bed

---
4. Shakespeare, *Hamlet*, 1.1.10.
5. Shakespeare, *Macbeth*, 1.3.48.
6. Shakespeare, *Macbeth*, 1.3.75.
7. Shakespeare, *Macbeth*, 1.7.32.

to ordering the assassination of a rival's wife and children. When he finally meets his own tragic end, his vicious ambition has deteriorated so far that nothing remains of his former courage but savage self-protection. "They have tied me to a stake; I cannot fly / but bear-like I must fight the course."[8] By the end Macbeth is brutal and bestial, his divided soul so pronounced that he is barely human.

Macbeth's downfall is marked by an excess of desire. He wants to advance his position, he wants to be king, he wants to prove his manhood to his wife, he wants to cover up his crimes, he wants to protect his stolen throne. He falls further and further into internal division as he denies his duty and elevates his desire. Interestingly, Macbeth is not blind to his own divided soul; he openly acknowledges it in Act I, Scene 7 when he deliberates about whether or not to kill Duncan:

> *He's here in double trust;*
> *First, as I am his kinsman and his subject,*
> *strong both against the deed; then, as his host,*
> *Who should against his murderer shut the door,*
> *Not bear the knife myself. Besides, this Duncan*
> *Has born his faculty so meek, hath been*
> *So clear in his great office, that his virtues*
> *Will plead like angels . . .[9]*

When he makes this speech, Macbeth is not yet fully

---

8. Shakespeare, *Macbeth*, 5.7.1-2.
9. Shakespeare, *Macbeth*, 1.7.12–20.

committed to his wicked plot, and he tries to fortify his desiring soul against vice with a list of his duties as a subject, a host, a patriot, and a moral agent. It nearly works; he resolves to "proceed no further in this business."[10] But duty goes to the wall when his wife appears.

One of the most memorable women in the history of literature, Lady Macbeth is a formidable desiring soul in her own right. She refuses to capitulate to Macbeth's claims of conscience, and she belittles his masculinity until he agrees to commit the murder.

What beast was't, then,
That made you break this enterprise to me?
When you durst do it, then you were a man;
And to be more than what you were, you would
Be so much more the man.[11]

Significantly, Lady Macbeth makes no attempt to answer Macbeth's moral qualms; she merely appeals to his appetites.

Art thou afeard
To be the same in thine own act and valor
As thou art in desire?[12]

Here she makes a direct appeal to his corrupt desire, urging him to abandon the duties that restrain him. Lady

---

10. Shakespeare, *Macbeth*, 1.7.31.
11. Shakespeare, *Macbeth*, 1.7.47–51.
12. Shakespeare, *Macbeth*, 1.7.39–41.

Macbeth embodies the diabolical Feminine, channeling her inherent power over her husband toward vice instead of virtue. Fair is foul, and foul is fair. Lady Macbeth renounces virtue entirely, tipping the scales toward division and destruction. These two desiring people quash all duties to fulfill their desires, aggravating their divided souls and sealing their doom.

Desire in itself is not wicked, but incomplete. Duty must harmonize the dissonance in the desiring soul, and Shakespeare presents a harmonious character who counterbalances Macbeth. Yes, Macbeth is a usurper, but since King Duncan is his first cousin, he has a legitimate, though distant, claim. And between Macbeth and the throne are three obstacles—Duncan and his two sons, Malcolm and Donalbain. After murdering Duncan, Macbeth frames the heirs, forcing them to flee under suspicion of murder, which leaves the throne vacant for Macbeth to seize for himself. The eldest and true heir, Malcom, escapes to England where he receives sanctuary at the court of King Edward the Confessor. This is a meaningful choice on Shakespeare's part because King Edward is a canonized saint. The message is subtle but straightforward—as the pretender Macbeth declines into madness in a hell of his own making, the true king Malcolm awaits justice in a sanctum of order and piety.

Back in Scotland, all is chaos. "Each new morn new widows howl, new orphans cry, new sorrows strike heaven on the face."[13] The Scottish nobles plot to overthrow Macbeth and restore the rightful king. A thane named Macduff volunteers to fetch Malcolm from the English court. In a strange

---

13. Shakespeare, *Macbeth*, 4.3.4–6.

but essential scene, Malcolm resists Macduff's urgent appeal to return to Scotland, citing that if he were to take the throne, "my poor country shall have more vices than it had before."[14] Macduff wants to know what he means, and Malcolm answers.

It is myself I mean, in whom I know
All the particulars of vice so grafted
That when they shall be opened black Macbeth
Will seem as pure as snow.[15]

Here he claims that he is too vicious to rule. First he says he is a sadistic womanizer. "Your wives, your daughters, your matrons, and our maids could not fill up the cistern of my lust."[16] Secondly he is so avaricious that he would plunder the nobles and people to fill his coffers. "My more-having would be as a sauce to make me hunger more."[17] Noble Macduff balks at the excesses of Malcolm's depraved desires, but considers them bearable trade-offs to depose Macbeth. But he draws the line at Malcolm's final declaration that he possesses no "king-becoming graces,"[18] and would "pour the sweet milk of concord into hell, uproar the universal peace, and confound all unity on earth."[19] A king who hates peace and desires division? A ruler not only governed by appetite, but preferring vice? Macduff has had enough.

---

14. Shakespeare, *Macbeth*, 4.3.48.
15. Shakespeare, *Macbeth*, 4.3.52-55.
16. Shakespeare, *Macbeth*, 1.7.62-64.
17. Shakespeare, *Macbeth*, 4.3.82.
18. Shakespeare, *Macbeth*, 4.3.93.
19. Shakespeare, *Macbeth*, 4.3.99-101.

Malcolm: If such a one be fit to govern, speak. I am as I have spoken.
Macduff: Fit to govern? No, not to live. O nation miserable . . . when shalt thou see thy wholesome days again?[20]

Macduff begins to rail against the heir's bad character and declares his intention to exile himself from Scotland forever. A land ruled by such kings is destined for ruin, and Macduff will not be a party to its destruction. At this Malcolm suddenly shifts ground.

Macduff, this noble passion,
Child of integrity, hath from my soul
Wiped the black scruples, reconciled my thoughts
To thy good truth and honor.[21]

Malcolm reveals that the bizarre conversation was a test to gauge Macduff's integrity. He admits he wanted to see how far Macduff would go to overthrow Macbeth, because he knows that a nobleman without moral limits can offer no meaningful service to an honorable king. Retracting his self-recriminations, he declares himself chaste, honest, frugal, loyal, and—most importantly—"my poor country's to command."[22] To Malcolm, kingship is a sacred trust, and he requires his thanes and generals to be men of integrity whose personal desires are subject to moral duties. Malcolm wants to be crowned Scotland's king, but in accor-

---

20. Shakespeare, *Macbeth*, 4.3.103-106.
21. Shakespeare, *Macbeth*, 4.3.115-118.
22. Shakespeare, *Macbeth*, 4.3.133.

dance with piety, integrity, and honor. His desire for the throne is properly ordered because it is harmonized with kingly virtues.

Macbeth and Malcolm both desire to rule, but Malcolm is a hero and Macbeth a villain. What ultimately separates the two is the question of duty: Malcolm unites duty with proper desire while Macbeth rejects duty to isolate disordered desire. And what about us? Through Malcolm's ruse we perceive that the dividing line between hero and villain is marginal, and anybody can go either way. Looking back, I wish my divided youthful self had been dutiful as well as desiring in my thwarted college romance. A unified soul would have recognized another woman's prior claim as a compelling obstacle to the object of desire. The paradox is that I would have loved that boy better (albeit differently) if I had and been more deserving of the love for which I longed. I would have been not only a better, but a happier, young woman if I had reckoned with duty before indulging desire. The contrast between Macbeth and Malcolm illuminates something essential about the desiring soul. Those of us who are led by longings must learn to be good before we can be happy. The pursuit of virtue is a necessary prerequisite for the good life. Without it, we are divided souls, inflicting ever increasing damage upon ourselves and others.

Christ speaks to the divided soul when he utters these terrible words:

> *If any man comes to me and hates not his father, and mother, and wife, and children, and brethren, and sisters, yea, and*

his own life also, he cannot be my disciple.[23]

But how do we reconcile this command with other words of Christ?

Ask, and it shall be given you; seek, and ye shall find; knock, and it shall be opened unto you: For every one that asks receives; and he that seeks finds; and to him that knocks it shall be opened.[24]

How can God withhold and fulfill at the same time? This is not a mere intellectual exercise, but a profound spiritual and existential dilemma. As I huddled on the stairs weeping for my lost children, how was it possible to embrace either of these sayings? On the one hand, how could I hate my own flesh, my own motherhood, my own lost and longed-for children? But on the other, how could I keep faith in a God who did not save me from this loss?

Author Graham Greene grapples with mysteries like these in his 1951 novel *The End of the Affair*. The chronicle of an aborted extramarital affair between the beautiful Sarah Miles and her lover, Maurice Bendrix, the novel ponders what happens when the desiring soul repudiates disordered desire. Sarah is an ardent woman living in an empty marriage with the dutiful civil servant, Henry Miles. She longs for intimacy and intensity, while Henry contents himself with systems and superficiality. Her fervent love affair with the amorous Maurice adds ardor to her drab existence.

---

23. Luke 14:26 (KJV).
24. Matthew 7:7-8 (KJV).

Henry offers duty; Maurice desire, and we wonder if the arrangement just might work. Why not two men for two needs? But when Maurice nearly dies in a London air raid, Sarah, an atheist, prays desperately, promising God that if He spares Maurice's life she will end the affair. "I'll give him up forever, only let him be alive with a chance."[25] Moments later, Maurice emerges unharmed from the rubble, and "now the agony of being without him starts, and I wished he was safely back dead again under the door."[26] But Sarah keeps her word. The remainder of the novel explores the irrevocable impact of the end of the affair for Sarah, Henry, and Maurice. At first, they all suffer. For months Sarah experiences depression, anxiety, listlessness, and irritability. Henry and Maurice become increasingly paranoid, both convinced that Sarah has taken another lover. But Sarah keeps her desperate promise, cutting off all contact with Maurice. Meanwhile she records her turmoil in her diary, which reveals a growing spiritual awareness. Her conversion is slow and arduous, but deeply, agonizingly real.

> *Dear God, I've tried to love and I've made such a hash of it. If I could love you, I'd know how to love them. I believe the legend. I believe you were born. I believe you died for us. I believe you are God. Teach me to love.*[27]

Sarah's conversion is an icon of the Prodigal's salvation. At great cost she strips away lesser loves and finds her way

---

25. Greene, *The End of the Affair*, 76.
26. Ibid.
27. Greene, *The End of the Affair*, 96.

to Love Itself. Painful self-denial becomes her pathway to God. Although passionate Maurice (desire) formerly satisfied her romantic yearnings while prosaic Henry (duty) discharged his marital requirements, the resulting fragmentation only deepened everyone's internal division. Duty and desire cannot be fulfilled in isolated categories; like the brothers in the parable, they cry out to be reconciled. The affair exacerbates the very wound they vainly attempt to heal. Healing begins in renunciation and continues in reconciliation. Sarah reminds us that God did not create us for schism, but for unity.

Like Christ, we all must carry a cross and walk the *Via Dolorosa*—the Way of Weeping. Sarah's way was ending the affair—ours must be our own. I lost a boy I thought I loved and relinquished my dream of having many children. It is not a sin to fall in love or to conceive many children, but ultimately my true desire is not these things at all. Instead my fundamental longing is for what the Eastern church calls *theosis*, or union with God. To be one with God means we must be at one with ourselves. We must be whole. When Eve bit into the forbidden fruit, she severed desire from duty, divided her soul, and fell from unity with God. It was a self-inflicted, mortal wound. As Proverbs 10:1 says, "a foolish woman tears down her house with her own hands." Such was Eve. Such was Sarah. Such is me. Sometimes our lesser loves, however holy in themselves, eclipse our vision of love itself and must therefore be removed—not as punishment, but as a means of salvation. Sarah's story vividly recounts the pain of that process. It feels like death, and indeed it is.

Soon after ending the affair, Sarah develops a cough. Two years later, Sarah is dead, and the men rage and grieve. But as her body deteriorates, her soul heals. By the time she dies, Sarah's Prodigal soul learns to attach to its true object: not a human lover, but the divine lover of her soul—Christ Himself. Instead of losing her ability to love Henry and Maurice, she begins to love them better. In Christ her human love becomes vibrant and deep and rich and full, pouring itself out to the suffering men in a new way. Sarah teaches us that the capacity to love like Christ is the glory of the desiring soul.

Sarah's love does not end at her death. Small but significant interventions take place in the lives of those left behind. Everybody who knew Sarah, including Maurice and Henry, experiences something unexplainable. Sarah desires their good from beyond the grave, continuing the ministry of love that began in herself. In the end readers are forced to reckon with their own preconceptions of Sarah's transformation.

Christ Himself died, and only through death can we fully participate in His life. But the story of salvation does not end at the cross; it consummates itself in the resurrection—the restoration of all things. Sarah dies to her distorted desire, and in so doing rises to their transformation and fulfillment. God does not rebuke but *responds* to the desperate pleas of her desires. Every excruciating moment of renunciation becomes a step forward on her healing journey. She is afraid it will tear her apart, but instead it knits her back together. Sarah longs for love, and in response love Himself appears, transfiguring the former damage of the affair into the healing of all three souls—a mighty and immense grace indeed.

And so it is with us. I give thanks that God in his mercy turned heaven into iron for me for a time. Unrequited desire taught me to cry out with Job, "though He slay me, yet I will trust Him."[28] Wendell Berry writes that the only real prayer is, "Thy will be done."[29] The pilgrimage of the desiring soul is renunciation, but always for the sake of joy. Self-denial is not an end in itself. We are not stoics; we are Christians. But for me it is a pagan story that best illuminates the robust glory of the desiring soul. The *Odyssey* is the story of a homecoming. Following the Trojan War, the embattled King Odysseus embarks on his journey to his native land to reunite with his wife, Penelope, and their son, Telemachus, who has never known his father. Odysseus has not seen his home or family in twenty years. In his absence a posse of violent and debauched suitors occupy the palace—dissipated young men who court the queen and plunder Ithaca's riches. His family and his land are in grave danger; the stakes are high, and their only hope is Odysseus' return.

Odysseus' homeward journey is fraught with both dangers and temptations. The dangers include monsters, shipwrecks, curses, storms, vengeful immortals—even a voyage into the land of death itself. The resourceful Odysseus is equal to it all. But the temptations are more insidious. The lotus flower of forgetful pleasures, the sirens who stroke his ego, the seductive sorceress who shares her bed, the

---

28. Job 13:15 (KJV).
29. Berry, *Jayber Crow*, 51.

enchanting goddess who promises immortality in her Aegean paradise, the rich king who offers his virgin daughter and succession to his wealthy throne. Any of these desirable detours could be his if he will only forsake his homeward quest. But Odysseus remains steadfast. When the beautiful goddess Calypso offers him eternal life if he will abandon his journey to remain in her smooth caves, Odysseus responds.

> Look at my wise Penelope. She falls far short of you,
> Your beauty, your stature. She is mortal after all
> And you, you never age or die.
> Nevertheless I long—I pine, all my days—
> to travel home and see the dawn of my return.
> And if a god will wreck me yet again on the wine-dark sea,
> I can bear that too, with a spirit tempered to endure.
> Much have I suffered, labored long and hard by now
> In the waves and wars. Add this to the total—
> Bring the trial on![30]

Odysseus is an icon of harmonious desire. Certainly it is his duty to return home, especially since the situation there is dire. But it is not duty that motivates Odysseus—it is desire. His love and longing for home forge "a spirit tempered to endure." His desiring soul remains fixed on its proper object, fortifying and ennobling him to overcome trials and temptations. When he finally rallies his loyal subjects, slays the wicked suitors, retakes his rightful throne, and embraces his beloved queen, he not only fulfills his

---

30. Homer, The *Odyssey*, 5.239-249.

long-delayed duties, but sates his long-denied desires. At the moment of their reunion, Penelope invites, "If it's bed you want, it's bed you'll have, whenever the spirit moves you."[31] From the throne-room to the bedroom, The *Odyssey* ends in the union of duty and desire in every realm of existence.

Like Odysseus, the pilgrimage of our souls is oriented homeward. Desire guides us to joy in the midst of our particular dangers and temptations. While I sat weeping on the stairs, I was close to despair. I wanted to shake my fist at God. *My* will be done, not thine. No dutiful platitude would comfort me, but God is beyond platitudes. In the valley of the shadow of death, new thoughts crept in. I wrapped my arms around my belly and remembered the travail of pregnancy, birth, and new life; I remembered my living children, Jack and Lucy. For the first time, I thought...What if I was never able to have children at all? What if I am barren and yet have borne children? What if my Jack and Lucy are two miraculous interventions of intervening grace? What then? Would I have eyes to see? Would I release my plans and receive the life I was given? Would I allow myself to lament but also to love? Would I accept with open hands that desire is full of endless distances, painful but holy? To this day I weep for my lost little ones. I light a candle for them at every church service—for Caleb, Susanna, James, Mary Constance, Henry, Marina, and, yes, Penelope, whose faces I will never behold this side of heaven. But like Odysseus, I am led homeward by my desire, beset by dangers and temptations, while, nevertheless, I long for my true home.

---

31. Homer, The *Odyssey*, 23.291-292.

3

THE GREATEST OF THESE IS LOVE

Love, Repentance, and Endurance

My first conscious memory of love is an interior debate I carried on with myself at the age of four on the subject of which parent I loved the most. On my mother's side were the salient points that she was—like me—a girl, that she had soft hands, and that she was shortly to provide me with a baby brother. On the other hand, my father was undeniably superior in the essential matters of hugs, tickles, patience, and asking "who's there" when I felt the urge to repeat hilarious knock-knock jokes. I puzzled over the question until it became insoluble, and then I climbed into my father's lap and snuggled into his chest while he wrapped his arms around me. In those years love was as unconscious as air. Like most children I was—regardless of the yet unknown frailties of my parents—beloved. And this undergirded everything.

Love is fundamental to human well-being. The Bible teaches that love covers a multitude of sins, and we see this in story after story: Princes and heroes kill dragons and monsters for love of their ladies; King Priam pleads for his son's body at the killer's feet; Mr. Darcy spurns social conventions for Lizzy Bennet's sake; David and Jonathan elevate their pact of friendship over their ambitions for power. In short, love is the dividing line of every enduring story in some essential way. But what does this have to do with duty and desire? The answer, of course, is everything because love is the only force that can heal our divided souls.

To demonstrate, we will look closely at examples of healing love from some beloved stories. Each contains iconic portrayals of division and restoration mediated by transformative love. Through them we envision our own stories as threads in a cosmic pattern of brokenness and repair. In this way literature is both a window and a mirror—a window into a world *beyond* ourselves and a mirror into the world of ourselves. It seems to me that this is the essential restorative capacity of fiction.

In these stories—as in all stories—love overcomes death, echoing the haunting poetry of the Song of Songs.

> *Love is as strong as death...*
> *Its flashes are flashes of fire,*
> *The very flame of the Lord.*
> *Many waters cannot quench love,*
> *Neither can floods drown it.*
> *If a man offered for love*
> *All the wealth of his house,*
> *He would be utterly despised.*[1]

---

1. Song of Songs 8:6-7 (ESV).

Love is as strong as death is a claim that should stop us in our tracks. It means that love and death are equally transformative and equally final. Both are irrevocable, changing us utterly and forever. Whatever is true of death is true of love, but reverted—death, so to speak, is "upside down" and love is "right side up." Divine Love created the world, death corrupted it, and love will save it. And since our souls are little worlds, love is the only remedy potent enough to mend our fractured psyches. King Solomon's poetry in Song of Songs is not hyperbole, but reality, elevating love to its proper place as the inflection point of our lives.

The pattern begins to weave itself in the very first story in Genesis. Biblical narratives like the creation story are more than historical fact; they also embody theology and enact truth. In the beginning God and His creation dwelled together in loving communion. When the serpent enticed Adam and Eve to break the commandment, Adam and Eve spurned the Divine Love that gave them life. With sin came death—a fundamental disruption so traumatic to life and order that death, both literal and metaphorical, still haunts the fragmented regions of every divided soul. But the story did not end there. Christ intervened to restore the life of the world through sacrificial love, uniting the division between duty and desire by keeping and fulfilling the law (duty) and inviting us to paradise (desire). To quote an ancient Christian liturgy, he "trampled down death by death" by resurrecting Himself from the grave. Love overcame death. This eternal tale is so fundamental to the fabric of the world that we cannot help but tell it over and over again in myth, epic, fairy tale, novel, and our own lives.

Consider, for example, *The Lord of the Rings*, J.R.R. Tolkien's three-part fantasy tale which contains an overt examination of the divided soul in Gollum (formerly Smeagol), whose internal division is so stark that the warring parts of his personality have different names. Gollum is a character so marked by degradation that we cannot imagine him as a whole person until he encounters Frodo, who shares his suffering and invites his divided soul to encounter its own brokenness and turn toward healing.

First named Smeagol, Gollum was once an ordinary hobbit. One birthday, long before the ring quest that is the plot of the novel, Smeagol goes fishing with his cousin, who finds a golden ring buried in the river muck. Smitten with the object, Smeagol demands it for his birthday present. His companion refuses, though, and, overcome by desire, Smeagol drowns him in the river and takes the ring for himself. The ring becomes his "precious," and its possession the dominating passion of his life. Smeagolcossets his precious as it slowly degrades him. Since the ring of power is an immortal object, Smeagol does not die, but degenerates, becoming vicious and bestial—the mark of the ring. In time, even Smeagol's physicality decays. More like a beast than a person, he forgets his own name and becomes known as Gollum after the gulping noise his throat makes as he swallows empty air—a manifestation of his inordinate hunger for the ring.

Gollum is so degraded by his centuries with the ring that he seems to lack any remnant of his former self. Surely there is nothing loveable about the wretched creature? When Frodo learns of Gollum's viciousness and treachery, he cries, "What a pity that Bilbo did not stab that wretched creature when he had a chance!"[2] But Gandalf the wise wizard rebukes him. "Pity? It was pity that stayed his hand! Pity, and Mercy: not to strike without need."[3] He declares that Bilbo, "Took so little hurt from the evil, and escaped in the end,"[4] because he began his ownership of the ring with an act of mercy. He urges Frodo to imitate Bilbo's mercy, declaring that "the pity of Bilbo may rule the fate of many —yours not least."[5]

Although he does not fully understand it, Frodo takes Gandalf's message to heart. But soon he feels the burden of the ring and deals gently with Gollum when circumstances unite them in the quest. By that time Frodo has carried the ring long enough to comprehend its malignancy, which increases his capacity for compassion. "Now that I see him," he tells his faithful companion, Sam, after they capture and subdue the spying Gollum, "I do pity him."[6] Following Bilbo's example, Frodo spares Gollum's life in exchange for an oath on the ring to lead them unharmed to Mordor. And then, in an act of mercy more profound than sparing his life, Frodo begins calling Gollum by his old name, Smeagol, evoking the tormented creature's true identity for the first time in centuries.

Once near the ring, Gollum's divided soul becomes radically visible. Duty to his oath rages against desire for the "precious." Switching between the two sides of his war-

---

2. Tolkien, *The Fellowship of the Ring*, 68.
3. Ibid.
4. Ibid.
5. Tolkien, *The Fellowship of the Ring*, 69.
6. Tolkien, *The Two Towers*, 222.

ring soul, his dutiful Smeagol-side is a fawning, obsequious creature who constantly craves affirmation. His desiring Gollum-side is cunning and manipulative, seeking to exploit Frodo's trust. As the companions approach Mordor, the two sides engage in open war, the Smeagol-side advocating for leniency on the "nice hobbit;" the Gollum-side scheming for the ring, chanting, "We wants it, we wants it, we wants it."[7] Frodo, embattled by the burden of the ring, is gentle with Gollum for the sake of Smeagol, but Sam remains suspicious. And for a long time, it is unclear which side of Gollum's divided soul will triumph. But one night, after showing the hobbits the way into Mordor, Smeagol watches Frodo while he sleeps:

> *Then he came back, and slowly putting out a trembling hand, very cautiously he touched Frodo's knee—but almost the touch was a caress. For a fleeting moment, could one of the sleepers have seen him, they would have thought that they beheld an old weary hobbit, shrunken by the years that had carried him beyond his time, beyond friends and kin, and the fields and streams of youth, an old starved pitiable thing.*[8]

In this weighty moment, Gollum's divided soul hangs in the balance. But Sam awakens, perceives Gollum hovering over Frodo, and lashes out. "What have you been up to—

---

7. Tolkien, *The Two Towers*, 241.
8. Tolkien, *The Two Towers*, 324.

sneaking off and sneaking back, you old villain?"[9]

And at this malediction, dutiful Smeagol in his intense fragility disappears forever, swallowed by desiring Gollum: "The fleeting moment had passed, beyond recall."[10]

This brief but tragic misunderstanding cements a chasm within Gollum, and in response, he rejects duty and enthrones the disordered desire for the ring as the malevolent king in his divided soul.

Perhaps it is tempting at this point to perceive desire as inherently wicked and duty as fundamentally righteous. Certainly this is a common perception, but it is too simplistic. Gollum's trajectory of deterioration is not an indictment of desire itself, but of bad desire—of the desire for the ring, which is, Tolkien affirmed, "an allegory . . . of Power (exerted for domination)."[11] The ring's corrupting power becomes so strong that healing requires radical re-unification. And that's why Frodo, a fellow ring-bearer, is perhaps Gollum's only possible savior. Like Gollum, Frodo carries a weight too great to bear, but he maintains his true identity. But how? He does so in two ways: through Sam, who loves him, and through the quest, which guides him. In other words, Frodo remains insulated from the full evil of the ring because he has something good to *want* (friendship and home) and something virtuous that he *ought* to do (complete the quest). The unity of desire-and-duty in the quest shields him from the lure of wicked power for a long time, and when Gollum joins the quest, he gains access to these

---

9. Ibid.
10. Ibid.
11. Tolkien, *The Letters of J.R.R. Tolkien*, Letter 186.

wholesome influences. In calling forth Gollum's lost name, Frodo opens the door to freedom, and it almost works.

Every time I read the story I dread this moment. I cannot help but imagine it as I wish it had happened—a pale dawn breaks as the vigilant Sam observes Gollum approaching Frodo, holding out his trembling hand. Sam sees that this vulnerable sufferer is a different creature than the sneaking wretch he expects. He recognizes that something is happening to Gollum, that his hand is reaching toward Frodo to connect, not to defraud. I imagine that Sam keeps silent, awaiting the awakening of grace, overcome with the sacred potential of the moment. Frodo opens his eyes to behold Smeagol as he could have been and as it is not yet too late for him to become. And although I know all of the redeeming moments to come in the story, I still wonder what would have happened for Gollum, for Frodo, for Sam, and for all of Middle Earth if Sam had held space that morning for Smeagol to touch Frodo.

But Sam's duty is to protect Frodo, and the stakes are too high for error. He neither recognizes nor trusts Gollum's bond with Frodo, which prevents him from seeing the unexpected workings of love. Sam suspects that Gollum will betray his duty to Frodo, but Gollum's potential for healing is not in fulfilling his oath, but in forming a relationship. In the spoiled moment of transformation, Sam curses Gollum just as a fragile love was dawning. The bond of shared suffering between the ring-bearers was nearly transfigured into something far more powerful. This moment contains the revelation of a deep mystery—even Gollum's ravaged soul could have been healed by the only force more potent than its desire for the ring, which is not duty after all, but *love*.

Gollum could not be saved by obligation. His oath on the ring was doomed from the start. Any covenant built on a wicked foundation necessarily fails because evil is too frail to uphold nobility. It was not his duty to his vow, but Frodo's forgiving love that was the true remedy. Through Frodo we see that it is relationship, not responsibility, that truly heals.

In this part of the story Frodo is a Christ-like figure to Gollum, dispensing grace as a co-sufferer of the same ailment. His sacrificial mercy begins to knit Gollum's fractured self together, small stitch by small stitch, until the ring's malignant power begins ever so slightly to wane.

So it is with us. Like Gollum, we are easily dominated by temptation, vacillating between the two sides of our conflicted inner beings as we stumble towards eternity. Only the voice of love calling out our lost names, our true selves—the forgotten Smeagols buried within us—evokes the possibility of inner reconciliation. But it remains a fragile and elusive possibility. Like Gollum, we must actively respond. This is the moment of reckoning, when we encounter love's transcendence and choose whether or not to turn towards it.

Gollum's resistance to love is tragically common, but the invitation itself remains universal. Everyone, no matter how despicable, encounters it. The invitation is so compelling that we have to ask ourselves why anybody would refuse it. The answer is that love is as costly to receive as it is to give. It is as strong as death. Death is a fundamental separation, but love is a radical reunification. Both alter us forever, which requires repentance.

How does repentance—a very theological word—relate to love and the divided soul? Repentance is the proper response to love's charity. Frodo's love alone is insufficient to heal the damage that Gollum inflicts. Gollum must change, which requires him first to repent.

Consider a similar connection between repentance and love in Fyodor Dostoevsky's Russian masterpiece, *Crime and Punishment*. I will declare immediately that Dostoevsky does not make love easy. The main character is Rodion Raskolnikov, a university student who brutally murders an old woman with an ax. Raskolnikov is a divided soul—his name comes from the Russian word *raskol*, which means *schism* or *split*—and throughout the story he vacillates wildly between extremes of goodness and depravity, rising to heights of magnanimity and generosity before falling to depths of cunning and betrayal, sometimes within moments.

Crime and Punishment contemplates what happens to a person who acts on depraved desires. Rather than the story of a murder, it is the story of a murderer whose labyrinthine inner life conveys the shadow-side of human nature. The dark landscape of Raskolnikov's divided soul is nearly unbearable without the glimmers of light emanating from its female protagonist, a young prostitute named Sonya whose profession feeds her impoverished family. Sonya is an icon of grace. Even her sexual servitude alerts us to her enduring posture of self-emptying care—she literally lays herself down for others.

Sonya's enormous capacity for sacrificial love is the novel's redeeming force. When she suspects Raskolnikov of the murder, she responds with compassion instead of recoiling in horror. "What have you done—what have you done to yourself!"[12] she said in despair, and, jumping up, she flung herself on his neck, threw her arms round him, and held him tight.

Sonya's words spring from the same spiritual vision as Frodo's. She sees beyond Raskolnikov's divided soul. Her compassion moves him to confide that he is the murderer. Psychologically tormented and physically ill, Raskolnikov is near to collapse.

> *"Such suffering!" Burst in a painful wail from Sonya.*
>
> *"Well, what do I do now, tell me!" He said, suddenly raising his head and looking at her, his face hideously distorted by despair.*
>
> *"What to do!" She exclaimed . . . "Go now, this minute, stand in the crossroads, bow down, and first kiss the earth you've defiled, then bow to the whole world, on all four sides, and say aloud to everyone: I have killed. Then God will send you life again. Will you go? Will you go?"*[13]

Sonya urges him to confess, to repent, to suffer, to put his trust in God. She does not coddle or enable him. Such love is what we call charity—it is neither erotic nor romantic, and it springs from her recognition that they are both

---

12. Dostoevsky, *Crime and Punishment*, 411.
13. Dostoevsky, *Crime and Punishment*, 420.

sinners in need of grace. Sonya stands against his justifications and absorbs his vitriol, showing mercy on his sins but demanding their renunciation. She prescribes the severe medicine of repentance to heal his self-inflicted malady.

It takes Raskolnikov a long time to confess. After he is convicted and imprisoned, Sonia follows him to Siberia where she dedicates herself to his salvation. Little by little Sonya's co-suffering love chips away at Raskolnikov's hard heart, and at last he flings himself down before her, weeping and repenting at her feet. "They were resurrected by love; the heart of each held infinite sources of life for the heart of the other."[14] In the end *Crime and Punishment* is not just a crime novel—it is a love story of divine charity.

Sonya and Frodo are literary shadows of Christ, the source of love. Frodo risks his life to offer Gollum his true identity. Sonya lays herself down in the posture of a fallen woman. Both are merciful and forgiving, and it is in them that Gollum and Raskolnikov's hopes of redemption converge.

Frodo and Sonya show us that the divided soul cannot rescue itself. Love must have an external source—it requires both subject and object, both lover and beloved. The response to such love is repentance, but repentance is not an end in itself. The true end of repentance is joy, as we see in the first words of St. John the Baptist in the gospel of Matthew: "Repent, for the kingdom of heaven is at hand."[15] What does it look like to embrace repentance and follow the path of change to its proper end? To contemplate how

---

14. Dostoevsky, *Crime and Punishment*, 549.
15. Matthew 3:2 (ESV).

love truly heals the divided soul, we turn to Charlotte Brontë's 1847 novel, *Jane Eyre*.

As a child, Jane is orphaned and unloved, which teaches her to loathe her cruel relations. At boarding school, she suffers from starvation, neglect, and abuse. Her life is marked by misery and hatred, but soon she finds consolation from a friend, Helen Burns, whose piety and stoicism awaken Jane's conscience. Their friendship sets Jane on a path of repentance that begins to temper her volatile nature with virtue. In a pivotal conversation, Jane confides the story of her impoverished childhood, expecting a sympathetic response. Instead Helen admonishes her to forgive. "She has been unkind to you, no doubt . . . Would you not be happier if you tried to forget her severity, together with the passionate emotions it excited?"[16] Helen's correction springs from kindness, and Jane softens. Like Frodo and Sonya, Helen sees who Jane could be, and her example moves Jane to reflect on herself. "I heard her with wonder: I could not comprehend this doctrine of endurance . . . I felt that Helen Burns considered things by a light invisible to my eyes. I suspected she might be right and I wrong."[17]

In her words Jane recognizes her divided soul and in her actions she finds a model of virtue to imitate. Crucially, Helen urges Jane to move past self-reflection and take action. When Jane expresses a resolve to take vengeance on her past oppressors ("when we are struck at without reason, we should strike back again very hard"[18]), Helen

---

16. Brontë, *Jane Eyre*, 69.
17. Brontë, *Jane Eyre*, 67.
18. Brontë, *Jane Eyre*, 69.

admonishes her to, "read the New Testament, and observe what Christ says, and how he acts; make his word your rule and His conduct your example."[19] But why? To what end? Helen reveals that too.

> *We are, and must be, one and all, burdened with faults in this world: but the time will soon come when, I trust, we shall put them off in putting off our corruptible bodies . . . I hold another creed: which no one ever taught me, and which I seldom mention; but in which I delight, and to which I cling: for it extends hope to all: it makes Eternity a rest . . . I live in calm, looking to the end.*[20]

Jane is amazed at Helen's "doctrine of endurance." Meeting her is the watershed moment of young Jane's life, and from her, Jane learns that repentance must lead to action if it is to lead to joy.

At eighteen, Jane leaves Lowood School to become a governess at Thornfield Hall, where she meets the mysterious and passionate Mr. Rochester. They fall in love. But forces stronger than social convention impede their union. As she stands at the altar on her wedding day, Jane discovers that Rochester is already married. In anguish, Rochester confesses that he kept the secret to keep Jane—his wife is wicked and insane, he declares. What is the harm in living as man and wife? He begs Jane to flout convention, but she refuses. Helen's pedagogy of virtue maintains its hold. Rochester's impassioned pleas and tender love break her

---

19. Ibid.
20. Brontë, *Jane Eyre*, 69-70.

heart but do not shake her resolve. Weeping, she cries:

> Laws and principles are not for the times when there is no temptation: they are for such moments as this, when body and soul rise in mutiny against their rigour . . . If at my convenience I might break them, what would be their worth?[21]

In agony but determined to maintain her moral duty, Jane flees into the wild Yorkshire moors and by the time she is taken in by strangers, she is nearly dead from starvation and exposure. She has no money, no friends, no resources, no prospects. Her courageous act of virtue has cost her everything, even to the brink of her life. For Jane, duty, so far, is death.

But that is not the end of Jane's story. As she recovers in the home of kind strangers, she becomes acquainted with St. John Elliot, a zealous young clergyman preparing to depart for the African mission field. He is handsome, intelligent, and devout. Perhaps St. John will offer Jane a second chance at love. But when St. John proposes, we see the dark side of the dutiful divided soul. "You were formed for labor, not for love," he tells her. "I claim you—not for my pleasure, but for my Sovereign's service."[22]

Yet Jane, who has nearly died for duty, recognizes that St. John is utterly wrong. "'Oh St. John,' I cried, 'Have some mercy!' I appealed to one who, in the discharge of what he believed to be his duty, knew neither mercy nor remorse."[23]

---

21. Brontë, *Jane Eyre*, 365.
22. Brontë, *Jane Eyre*, 464.
23. Ibid.

Jane recognizes that it is not duty, but duty divorced from desire, that is the true death. This spiritual truth is mirrored in her physical body. Jane is frail; her physique will not survive the African heat. If she marries St. John, she knows she will die in the Congo. Both spiritually and physically, she annihilates herself if she renounces her desire for Mr. Rochester in order to live by duty devoid of love.

Metaphorically, Jane dies twice: once to Rochester's desire without duty and once to St. John's duty without desire. But which death stays in the grave and which is resurrected? The answer, of course, is determined by love. At one point Jane nearly acquiesces to St. John, but at the critical moment she hears Rochester's voice calling for her across the moors. Once again love summons her beyond herself—the first time to death, but this time to life. She returns to Thornfield where she finds Rochester frail but free, the obstacles to their union resolved, and the man himself repentant and humble. His love for Jane and his sufferings for her sake have purified him. Finally Jane and Rochester unite duty and desire at the altar, and she utters her famous declaration of hard-fought joy: "Reader, I married him."[24]

Jane shows us how to live in the paradox of love and death. Love heals the divided soul, but love and death are mysterious companions. To love one another we must die to ourselves. At the time we feel like Jane, nearly dead on the moors, but the story does not end there. The wilderness is a necessary but temporary stop along the pilgrim way. The therapeutic culture of the divided world tells us to flee

---

24. Brontë, *Jane Eyre*, 517.

from the cost of love, but that is a lie. Every one of us must lay our lives down like Frodo, Sonya, and Jane. We all must suffer the wounds of love in order to be healed by it.

On the other hand, we are also all Gollum and Raskolnikov, divided within ourselves. We each coddle a "precious" that keeps us from joy. Like Eve, we, too, would have seized the forbidden fruit. It is only when we know that about ourselves, when we stand in the crossroads and declare ourselves murderers, when we reach our trembling hands toward the One who calls us by our true names, when we flee into the wilderness to escape our disordered loves, can we be saved. The Scriptures say truly that love is as strong as death, but only because it resurrects death. Love is the death of death.

4

A NOBLE TELOS

Marriage and Comedy

When I met Scott I was on shaky ground. Fresh from my bad college romance and other griefs, I was beginning to walk toward goodness, but I was unsteady on my feet. When a tall, auburn-haired stranger with his steadfast gaze offered me a ride home on his motorcycle and subsequently invited me to dinner, I had no idea how to be happy, but I knew he made everybody around him laugh. He took me hiking on our third date, and I was so nervous that I tripped over the rocks (multiple times), but he reached for my hand to steady me—and he hasn't let go since. Through our marriage, Scott teaches me to take joy seriously because, as Aristotle wrote, happiness is "the best, noblest, and most complete thing."[1]

I have a friend who comments that in marriage one spouse often makes the other happy, while one makes the other good. Happy and good. Duty and desire. Although

---

1. Aristotle, *Nicomachean Ethics*, 1097b20–1098a20.

this is too simplistic to be syllogistic, there's truth in it. Marriage unites two divided souls. We all know too much about earthly marriage to believe it is the solution to the problem of the divided self, but we can see how it is an icon of wholeness. Marriage is the union of duty and desire. In marriage my desire for my beloved is sanctified by my duty to him, and my desire for him transforms that duty into delight. When I violate duty or abandon desire, my marriage sickens, aggravating the breach between duty and desire. Because it is so powerful, it is also vulnerable. Every marriage treads the razor's edge between healing or harming the divided souls of man and wife, thus dividing their union. It is no wonder that marriage is a primary preoccupation of the stories we tell.

In the literary sense, the proper ending of a comedy is marriage and of tragedy, death. Reasons for this are not merely formal. Instead, comedy and tragedy weave throughout the cosmic order. Significantly, comedies in the literary sense do not culminate primarily in individual well-being, but in sacramental union. Happiness, it turns out, is inherently communal. But a tragedy ends in death, which is separation of the soul from the body. If marriage is the integration of two into one, death is the disintegration of one into less-than-one. Death and marriage are opposites. This is why hell is depicted as eternal death, and heaven as the marriage feast of the Lamb. This certainly does not mean that we have to be married in order to be happy or good—we know too much about fallen marriage to believe that. But it does mean that earthly marriage is a metaphor for the heavenly Real Thing. Marriage was implemented from the foundation of the world as an ennobling institution reflecting and foreshadowing the final eschatological union between Christ and the Church. Marriage is our eternal destiny, which makes it the most natural and noble *telos* (Greek for purpose, aim, ultimate end) of the world's best stories.

The tale of creation culminates in a wedding, teaching us much about the nature of comedy. We have already examined how Adam and Eve's disobedience fractured the order of creation, which was created wholly harmonious. God created Adam and Eve male and female, demonstrating that masculinity and femininity are complementary cosmic realities enfleshed in men and women. Men did not invent masculinity nor women femininity. Gender is eternal, and men and women incarnate it just as water incarnates wetness. Together the two become one in marriage, instituted by God to join the masculine Man with the feminine Woman. Marriage is the crown of the created order, a microcosm of the world's original harmony embodied in human relationship.

But there is more to the story than its intended happy ending. God gave Adam and Eve three commands: to eat freely of every tree in Eden, to be fruitful and multiply and fill the earth, and to take dominion over the created order. Notice that they are not merely *allowed* to fulfill these joyful charges, but *commanded* to do so. In other words, Adam and Eve's ordained duties were to fulfill their inherent desires to eat, multiply, and rule. Duty and desire united in harmony. Quite literally, such a life is paradise.

But the serpent undermined Eve's duty to abstain from

the one tree, inflaming her desire to eat from it. She faced a choice to trust the created unity of duty and desire or to sever the bond. When Eve bit into the forbidden fruit, she severed the internal cohesion of her soul, dividing duty from desire and inflicting a primal wound soon mirrored by her husband. Scripture tells us that Adam was with her at the time of her temptation and that "Adam was not deceived."[2] He witnessed the serpent tempting his wife, recognized its lies, and failed to intervene. Like Eve, Adam also faced the choice to trust the created unity of duty and desire or to sever the bond by abdicating his duty. He, too, ate the fruit, cementing the breach between duty and desire for both genders. That is when tragedy—which is not a thing in itself but a decline from the created order—entered the world.

Tragedy is the irreparable severing of the human from God, the self, and one another. And the first interpersonal relationship to be corrupted by sin was marriage. Stories retell this traumatic archetypal rupture over and over again, from the embattled Odysseus—cursed by the gods, battling monsters and temptresses to reunite with his lonely bride—to the tragic Anna Karenina, whose calamitous beauty led to adultery and an ensuing slough of griefs. This has led many to conclude that the impulse of the cosmos tends toward tragedy.

But does the story of the first marriage have a tragic end? At first blush it appears so. After the couple ate the fruit, God offered Adam and Eve the opportunity to freely confess, but they refused, casting blame on one another instead. Adam

---

2. 1 Timothy 2:14 (KJV).

blamed "the woman Thou gavest to be with me,"[3] abdicating his duty to his wife and to the created order. Implicit in his words is an accusation against God. No longer is she "bone of my bone and flesh of my flesh;"[4] she is merely "the woman," or the problem God thrust upon him. As Adam manifests his fallen masculinity, he displaces the culpability of his failure. And thus begins the long trail of aggression, passivity, sloth, fantasy, domination, and withdrawal that plagues the masculine soul.

On the other hand, Eve blames the serpent, who "beguiled me, and I did eat."[5] Eve attempts to absolve herself by claiming deceivability as an excuse for disobedience. By indicting the monster rather than herself, she enthrones her perceptions above God's design. Her words also carry an embedded accusation against God. If His terms had been more appealing than the serpent's temptations, she would not have fallen. She does not mention Adam at all—not to protect him, but to bypass him. Before He created Eve, God gave Adam the authority to protect and preserve the created order, but Eve heeds the serpent instead. These actions are at the root of many feminine vices: vanity, manipulation, gullibility, gossip, petulance, seductiveness, self-worship, and a controlling or critical spirit.

Together Adam and Eve, each in their own way, rupture the concord of duty and desire in themselves, and, by extension, throughout the whole created order. When we read stories about marriage, we instinctively respond to

---

3. Genesis 3:12 (KJV).
4. Genesis 2:23 (KJV).
5. Genesis 3:13 (KJV).

them as icons of either the comedy or the tragedy of the whole world. Creation was designed to be a comedy. Adam and Eve were created holy and whole in sacramental union and cosmic harmony, but they declined into recognizable destructive patterns that manifest in individuals, families, and societies.

Let us look at an example of this dynamic between men and women. Published in 1945, *That Hideous Strength* is the final novel in Lewis' theological science fiction trilogy. The central characters are Mark and Jane Studdock, a young married couple emblematic of modernity. Married for only six months, their bond is already crumbling. In the years following World War II a global crisis is imminent as the diabolical National Institute for Coordinated Experiments (N.I.C.E.) gains power in England, and the couple becomes entangled in the encroaching conflict. The ambitious Mark is recruited by the N.I.C.E. to participate in its propaganda campaign. Meanwhile, the icily self-protective Jane is invited to join a small band of freedom-loving citizens gathered at St. Anne's estate in the English countryside to await celestial guidance that will enable them to take down the N.I.C.E. They go their separate ways—Mark to the N.I.C.E. and Jane to St. Anne's—each nursing grievances.

The heart of the novel is the healing of the Studdock's divided marriage, which reflects the pervasive erosion of the surrounding zeitgeist. Both are products of their time, their generation, and their selfishness, manifesting the patterns of divided gender that began with Adam and Eve.

The novel opens with Jane's bitter disappointment that marriage has not provided "the mutual society, help, and comfort that the one ought to have of the other."[6] These words from the Anglican marriage service, first heard during their wedding six months earlier, have "stuck in her mind."[7] But significantly, the words Jane remembers reflect only the third purpose for matrimony in the Anglican rite. The first two—the procreation of children and the restraint of sin—make no impression on Jane's self-centered and secular mind. Since neither Jane nor Mark believe in the reality of sin nor plan to have children, the purpose of their marriage can only be the third and most self-oriented priority of marriage. In other words, Jane believes that marriage exists to make her happy but not to make her good.

In fact, Jane resents the cost of marriage to her daily life, her career, and her body. Feeling slighted, she invents petty punishments—rigid body language, aloof avoidance, pointed remarks, and martyred posturing. As Mark's frailties become more visible in the intimacy of marriage, she judges him. Nursing a sense of her own superiority, she accumulates a record of wrongs, concludes that her marriage has failed, and determines to construct a separate life. In this manner she reflects the sins of Eve, who justified her disobedience by denying responsibility, externalizing blame, and rejecting her husband.

However, at St. Anne's Jane encounters a new paradigm of communal harmony. Here the men and women acknowledge, even welcome, their differences and organize the household accordingly. For example, the men and women share the housework, but work on alternate days. "There

---

6. Lewis, *That Hideous Strength*, 11.
7. Ibid.

are no servants here," Jane is told, "and we all do the work. The women do it one day and the men the next."[8] Why? Because "men and women can't do housework together without quarreling."[9] Whatever we may think of the specific assertion (and don't dismiss it out of hand), this rule of life assumes a humane and communal vision of the differences between genders. What would happen if we approach gender differences frankly and graciously, dividing necessary work in a manner that dignifies one another with the aim of fruitful work?

The members of the household take the division of labor lightly, teasing one another gently: "It doesn't do to look at the cups too closely on the men's day,"[10] and "the cardinal difficulty in collaboration between the sexes is that women speak a language without nouns."[11] If St. Anne's is a microcosm of the world, Lewis offers a compelling alternative to the gender wars. Nobody at St. Anne's is perfect, but even as they spar, they treat one another with mutual respect and deference. Is it possible to dwell communally side-by-side as fully masculine and feminine beings without bitterness or accusation? St. Anne's does its best to figure out how.

As Jane witnesses the cheerful harmony between men and women at St. Anne's, her frigid exterior begins to thaw. And here Lewis does something peculiarly subtle. Jane's vision for goodness develops, but she remains critical of Mark. Though her eyes are opened to a better way, she con-

---

8. Lewis, *That Hideous Strength*, 164.
9. Ibid.
10. Ibid.
11. Ibid.

tinues to condemn Mark for falling short and even begins to wonder if her induction into St. Anne's is her ticket out of her marriage. Perhaps Mark is too far gone to be a part of her new life, especially since St. Anne's is a bastion of resistance against everything Mark stands for at the N.I.C.E. Maybe St. Anne's is rescuing her *from* her marriage, not *for* it.

Jane's point of view is bolstered by Mark's crumbling moral boundaries. At the N.I.C.E. headquarters at Belbury, Mark becomes increasingly acclimated to the dehumanizing and destructive atmosphere. Just as Jane experiences an ennobling catechesis at St. Anne's, so Mark undergoes a diabolical one at Belbury. At first he is not wicked, just weak. Slowly the N.I.C.E. unfolds its unholy intent, exploiting Mark's passivity and ambition until he is fully ensnared in its schemes. Along the way he occasionally exhibits ineffectual resistance but soon capitulates. He becomes a heavy drinker and avoids contact with anybody and anything that awakens his conscience— including Jane. His thoughts about Jane alternate between lust and rage. Without attempting to earn her respect, he fantasizes about convincing her to support or even admire him.

But it gets worse. Soon the N.I.C.E. leadership orders Mark to bring Jane to Belbury. In a dim part of his psyche he recognizes that the N.I.C.E. intends to harm his wife, but he is so conditioned and entrapped that he allows his mind to generate placating lies. Somehow it is Jane's fault that he lacks the courage to protect her. Somehow he is justified in sacrificing principle for power and profit.

The sins of Adam are evident in Mark. He refuses to

resist encroaching evil, thereby becoming a tool by which evil extends its reach. He abdicates his duty to his bride, desiring to enjoy her without serving her. Having already violated a myriad of moral boundaries, Mark is primed to voluntarily deliver his own wife to her destruction to protect and promote himself. He blames the very person he fails to protect.

Every marriage is plagued by the corruption of masculinity and femininity enacted in the Fall. But, of course, these sins are not limited to marriage. They plague other relationships too. Men and women continue to wound one another. Contemporary feminism disdains men as Jane disdains Mark. A gamut of influences ranging from so-called "purity culture" to ubiquitous pornography objectify women as Mark does Jane. Social forces exploit women and pervert men. We live out St. Paul's warning in Galatians 5:15: "If we bite and devour one another, take heed that ye be not consumed one to another."

Any ideological framework that casts masculinity or femininity as problems to be solved rather than realities to be revered is not only flawed, but diabolical. Masculinity and femininity predate the fall. They are inherently good. Our enemy is no man or woman, but the accuser who separated us from one another in the first place. Conflict between the genders is a wound of our divided souls, and further division will only aggravate it. Christians who deepen the wedge between the genders serve the monster, not the healer. But what is the healing response?

When Jane begins to wonder if Mark's moral failures will release her from her marriage, she speaks to Dr. Ransom, the wise leader of the St. Anne's cohort. She hopes for permission to extricate herself from her duty to Mark, but Ransom gently corrects her. "You do not fail in obedience through lack of love, but have lost love because you never attempted obedience."[12]

Love and obedience. Duty and desire. It is important to note that Dr. Ransom is not advocating direct obedience to Mark, for Mark is unworthy of it—after all, he is ready to deliver her to the N.I.C.E. Mark has abdicated his duty to Jane, and Ransom provides shelter from him. But that does not nullify her duty to obey Love itself, for love is the healing of the divided soul. Jane's only chance for healing is to freely obey the Divine Love that created her and Mark. Jane must learn that God's love extends even to Mark and that their marriage is fundamental to their healing. Neither Jane nor Mark (nor any married person) will be saved without reckoning with the spiritual state of the other, because in marriage two are one.

Eventually Jane begins to realize that her duty to Mark transcends her desire to be married to him. She recognizes for the first time that she is a person under authority, that the terms of marriage are absolute, and that her spiritual state cannot be extricated from the holy sacrament. This is a hard teaching for a woman steeped in modernity, and Jane resists. It is especially difficult because Jane's grievances against Mark are legitimate, and because she has begun a new and meaningful life without him. Is it not asking too much? Is it not too cruel, too demanding? Is this not love, but death? And yet in the very moment of painful reali-

---

12. Lewis, *That Hideous Strength*, 145.

zation, Jane simultaneously experiences something wholly new.

> *"Are you unhappy now?" said the Director. A dozen affirmatives died on Jane's lips as she looked up in answer to his question. Then suddenly, in a kind of deep calm, like the stillness at the centre of a whirlpool, she saw the truth, and ceased at last to think how her words might make him think of her, and answered, "No."*
>
> *"But," she added after a short pause, "it will be worse now, if I go back."*
>
> *"Will it?"*
>
> *"I don't know. No. I suppose not." And for a little time Jane was hardly conscious of anything but peace and well-being, the comfort of her own body in the chair where she sat, and a sort of clear beauty in the colours and proportions of the room.*[13]

When Jane opens herself to the possibility of submitting her will, not to Mark, but to the harmony of the cosmic order itself, she experiences herself as part of that harmony. The dissonance she had felt before her conversation with the Director was due not only to the disorder of her life, but of her soul. Although Jane was not wrong about Mark, she was wrong in *herself*, struggling vainly to escape from the

---

13. Lewis, *That Hideous Strength*, 143-144.

order of the world rather than to live according to it. Jane begins to consider that perhaps she belongs to her marriage as a normative sacramental reality. More slowly she comes to know that her obedience to the world as God made it will not harm her, but heal her.

Meanwhile, Mark is confronted with his failure as a husband through Dr. Dimble, one of the St. Anne's cohort. Mark approaches Dimble to discover Jane's whereabouts, but Dimble refuses to disclose the location. For just a moment, Mark's fogged vision clears and he recognizes himself as a coward and a villain. He sees that he is sitting face-to-face with a man who is doing what Mark ought to be doing—protecting Jane—and that he himself is the threat from which she must be protected. This moment of painful self-reflection blossoms into a flash of true repentance which catalyzes Mark's restoration.

But soon Mark faces a new temptation. Leadership at the N.I.C.E. decides to groom him for induction into their secret demonic rites. Imprisoned and alone, Mark finally realizes their wickedness and begins to summon the strength and resolve to resist. The N.I.C.E. runs Mark through a battery of psychological and spiritual torments designed to desensitize him to depravity. The plan backfires when Mark witnesses the full extent of their immorality. The N.I.C.E has overplayed its hand. The scales fall from his eyes, and for the first time he actually wants to flee temptation and embrace virtue. When ordered to desecrate a crucifix as part of his initiation, Mark finally shows himself a man. "I'll be damned if I do any such thing,"[14] he announces, a

---

14. Lewis, *That Hideous Strength*, 334.

statement as literal as it is idiomatic. In this moment of decisive action, Mark declares his allegiance to a spiritual goodness beyond himself, producing in earnest a true restoration of his corrupted masculinity. One of Adam's sins in Eden was to stand aside when meaningful action was required, and every man from that day to this must declare himself boldly at a moment of testing in order to heal the enduring wounds of the masculine soul.

In another transformative moment later in the story, Mark reflects on his clumsiness and selfishness in the bedroom, acknowledging that his sexual advances were intrusive and boorish because he thought only of himself. He does not mean this merely in terms of mutual pleasure in the act, but because it is analogous to his posture of self-indulgence rather than self-giving. As he confronts his own unworthiness, he grieves that he once took marital intimacy lightly. He ought to have cherished the marriage bed as a sacred bond and Jane as a precious trust. In proper shame he considers Jane as better than himself and resolves to set her free if he has hurt her too deeply to be forgiven. His humility confirms his restored masculine sexuality. Instead of desiring Jane to slake his appetites, he desires to make himself worthy of her. For the first time his desire for his wife activates his sense of duty to her. He understands that he must earn her respect in order to awaken her response. In this moment Mark demonstrates that the proper function of masculine desire is to ennoble a man to fulfill his masculine duty. Mark begins to imitate Christ, who lays down His life for His bride.

Each of these insights lead to transformative repentance and decisive action that restore Mark's true masculinity and Jane's true femininity. The diabolical plan of the N.I.C.E. ultimately fails to ruin them because despite their best efforts, the demonic forces cannot fully corrupt the goodness of gender. Mark eventually repents *because* he is a man, not in spite of it. The N.I.C.E. pushed him too far past the boundaries of his inherently good masculine identity, and he revolts, turning towards authentic manhood. His masculinity, although shaken, stands firm. The same is true of Jane. By the time they are reunited at St. Anne's, they are transfigured from their former shallow egoism to their deeper, truer selves, capable of virtues that will nourish their union—repentance, humility, courage, forgiveness, loyalty, wisdom, and, above all, selfless love. *That Hideous Strength* is a comedy that ends not with a wedding, but a marriage. What seemed at the beginning doomed to tragedy became a comedy.

Like *That Hideous Strength*, the story of the world is not tragic, but comic. St. Paul tells us that the whole creation groans and travails in longing for the revealing of the children of God. Our deepest desire is to return to Eden. In a previous novel, *Perelandra*, Dr. Ransom lives in paradise while on an interplanetary journey to Venus where he suffers to preserve the innocence of an unfallen world. When he beholds Venus' first Man and Woman, he falls at their feet. "Do not move away, do not raise me up," he says, "I have never before seen a man or a woman. I have lived all my life among shadows and broken images."[15] You and I are broken images of men and women. When we tell the

---

15. Lewis, *Perelandra*, 176.

stories of men and women "living happily ever after," we are, in a sense, returning to paradise.

Mark and Jane's marriage is an icon of intervening grace between men and women. Their story embodies the healing of duty and desire through the comic impulse of sacramental union. This is a bigger, deeper conception of comedy than mere satire or farce, and it is the form and structure of all true happy endings in literature and life. Comedy is therefore the truer story. Tragedy is only disrupted comedy—a story that breaks off in the middle. The Studdocks' restored marriage is a literary depiction of the reconciliation of male and female that will characterize the human return to paradise. The end of all apparent tragedies will give way to inevitable comedy, and the only question will be on which side of the resolution we find ourselves.

In one of His most poignant parables, Jesus tells us that "the kingdom of heaven is like unto a certain king, which made a marriage for his son."[16] The king invited guests to the feast, but they made excuses and refused to come. Finally the king sent his messengers to "the streets and lanes of the city"[17] to invite the poor, the orphaned, the maimed, the lame, and the blind. All are welcome to the wedding feast, but we must come of our own free will. This invitation echoes in our divided souls. It is the noble *telos* for which we are created and the happy ending of every story.

---

16. Matthew 22:2 (KJV).
17. Matthew 22:9 (KJV).

5

THE TURNING OF THE WHEEL

Death and Tragedy

In speaking of tragedy, I remember my mother. She was in many ways a heroic woman. Her father—my grandfather—was a brilliant but often brutal atheist, and my grandmother was a glittering, distant, emotional timebomb. The results were predictable. My mother, the youngest of three troubled siblings, grew up lonely and bewildered. Sometimes I play her early life like a film in my mind, flickering scenes she told me about from her childhood. I see her in a wide-angle shot, tiny and tow-headed, riding her bike alone down a desert road toward a jagged horizon. In my imagination I have dressed her in cut-off denim shorts and a brown-and-white striped T-shirt. Nobody knows where she is, the sun beats down on her bobbed hair, and her knobby knees are pumping up and down while the camera zooms in on tears streaming down her swollen face. The scene cuts to a shaky shot of my grandfather concurrently beating and belittling the cringing, pleading little boy who is my uncle while my mother, in the abject simplicity of childhood, flees as far as she can.

In another scene, the camera focuses peacefully on the (yellow?) front door of a (light blue?) suburban home. I think there should be honeysuckle vines growing over white porch rails. Suddenly the door bursts open and a little girl—my mother—rushes into the street, searching wildly for help. Her hands claw at her throat. Her mouth gapes and her chest heaves but no sound emerges. Her eyes bulge and her lips take on a blue tinge. Nobody notices. In another minute she takes a rasping, shuddering breath. The ice cube she choked on begins to melt, and she returns to the empty house and closes the door behind her. The camera rests on the closed door. And, scene.

It is understood, then, that my mother suffered, and her rage and fragility were surely predictable. As I said, it was heroic of her to survive, let alone to become a Christian at age fifteen, marry a devout evangelical seminarian, and raise three children in a household of faith. But the wheel of childhood trauma turns. If I, in turn, was lonely and bewildered, if I fled from home to shelter under the white lilac bushes lining our suburban cul-de-sac, if I shouldered the weight of generational grief when I was too young to understand or forgive it, then I am one of the vast assembly of wounded human souls who have not only read about, but *lived* in tragedy.

Tragedy, like comedy, is a cosmic reality. Unlike comedy, however, it is neither natural nor inevitable. As presented in the previous chapter, history is a comedy, unfolding from created perfection to the fall's disruption to the incarnation, life, death, and resurrection of Christ to the hope of heaven, where we will behold the reconciliation of all things in Christ. This is the *telos* of the created order. Comedy is therefore the truer story, which raises the question: how are we supposed to understand tragedy? Why tell sad stories at all?

The tragic genre exists because of the fall. If Adam and Eve had not transgressed, surely humans would have developed a rich storytelling tradition, but I have no idea what the stories would have been about. What would an unfallen story contain? We will never know, because art imitates life, and the only life we know is riddled with sin and suffering. Thus tragedy explores the disruption of the cosmic order, which means that all tragic narratives haunt the rupture between duty and desire. We were made for paradise, and we are forever reeling from the immensity of the damage of the divided soul. We tell sad stories in an endless lament for what we have lost and in a constant pursuit to comprehend the incomprehensible.

Aristotle, history's first literary critic, gave us the original meta-analysis of narrative in *Poetics*, his treatise on Greek drama. He claims that tragedy is storytelling's highest form because it can elevate the soul above human misery by enacting and purifying it. He invented the category of literary tragedy, which is characterized by a protagonist of great social and moral stature who undergoes a profound and disastrous fall. Famously, he writes that witnessing this tragic fall should provoke *catharsis*—a release of pity and fear that purges and uplifts the soul. It is in reference to this form of literary tragedy that Aristotle makes his famous claim that art imitates life, a process he calls *mimesis*. But *mimesis* is not realism. Aristotle believed that storytelling should imitate life as it *should be*, not as it is. Art is mimetic, he argues, in so far as it portrays the deeper truth of the human condition. That truth, according to Aristotle, is best explored in tragedy.

If this is so, we should be able to identify the breach between duty and desire in all tragic narratives. Consider Euripedes's drama, *Hippolytus*, which opens with a speech by Aphrodite, who is often identified as the goddess of love. But this is a misnomer. Aphrodite incites sexual passion, not love, and very rarely in the whole canon of Greek myth does that passion lead to any meaningful human happiness. In the case of *Hippolytus*, Aphrodite's opening speech is characteristic—she declares her intention to punish the eponymous Hippolytus, a handsome young nobleman. But why? Aphrodite usually favors young men, but Hippolytus is unusual. His "crime" is that he eschews erotic desire, reverencing chastity and dedicating himself to the service of Artemis, the virgin goddess. What's more, the young man himself is the fruit of disordered desire: his father, Theseus, king of Athens, raped his mother, the Amazon queen Hippolyta, after defeating the Amazons in battle. Asserting her erotic dominance, Aphrodite reveals her plan of vengeance against a young man who scorns her seductive power. In her speech she declares her scheme to awaken an illicit desire for Hippolytus in his stepmother, Phaedra, which will stir Theseus to kill him in retribution. She considers Theseus and Phaedra collateral damage. "Phaedra, noble as she is, shall nonetheless die," she pronounces, "I do not set such store by her misfortune as to let my enemies off from such penalty as will satisfy my heart."[1]

One eternally fascinating element of Greek tragedy is the complex interaction of fate and free will. Through no fault of her own, Phaedra is cursed by overwhelming lust for her stepson, but the action she takes as a result is entirely her own choice. A noble woman who is grievously tormented by her desire, she attempts, at first, to control her passion.

> *When love wounded me, I considered how I might bear it most creditably. My starting point was this, to conceal my malady with silence. For the tongue is not to be trusted: it knows well how to admonish the thoughts of others but gets from itself a great deal of trouble. My second intention was to bear this madness nobly, overcoming it by means of self-control.*[2]

But she fails. Desire for Hippolytus maddens and sickens her. Overcome by lust and shame, she cannot eradicate her desire with dutiful intentions, and "when with these means [she] was unable to master Aphrodite, [she] resolved on death."[3] She hangs herself, an act of free will. Even beyond death, her actions deepen the tragic duty/desire dichotomy of the play. In order to protect her reputation as a dutiful wife and her legacy as a dutiful queen, she leaves a suicide note accusing Hippolytus of rape. As she prepares for death, she soliloquizes that she is a queen and Hippolytus is only a bastard, and that after she is gone Theseus, their

---

1. Euripides, *Hippolytus*, 45-50.
2. Euripides, *Hippolytus*, 390-400.
3. Euripides, *Hippolytus*, 400.

land, and their children must be protected. All of this she admits frankly on stage, while keeping silent about any personal motive. There is no hint in her words that she hates Hippolytus for her lust and his virginity, but it is difficult to avoid interpreting her actions through that lens. The strange constellation of Phaedra's irreconcilable duties and desires raises many questions. Which is stronger—Phaedra's sense of duty or her cursed desire? Is it disordered duty or demented desire that motivates her death? Was there ever any hope that her divided soul could be healed?

Tragedy soon overtakes Hippolytus and Theseus. When Theseus finds the suicide note on his wife's corpse, he believes his wife's accusation. The young man presents the truth to his father in the most moving terms. He pleads for time to prove his innocence and begs his father to investigate the matter himself, swearing a sacred oath that he will not be found guilty. His argument is compelling, provoking the chorus to reply, "You have made a sufficient rebuttal of the charge against you by giving your oath in the name of the gods, which is no slight assurance."[4] But Theseus will not relent. He denounces him, declaring, "Your high and holy manner will be the death of me!"[5] He calls upon the god Poseidon, who once promised him three curses, to put Hippolytus to death. "But, father Poseidon, with one of the three curses you once promised me to kill my son, and may he not live."[6]

---

4. Euripides, *Hippolytus*, 1036-1037.
5. Euripides, *Hippolytus*, 1064.
6. Euripides, *Hippolytus*, 887-889.

Theseus' rage is understandable, but complicated because he himself raped Hippolytus' mother, also a queen, and the play implies that one of Hippolytus' motives for remaining a virgin was the outrage perpetrated against his mother. "O unhappy mother, O birth that gave no pleasure, may no one I love ever be a bastard!"[7] Hippolytus' very existence springs from his father's violent desire and violated duty. He has tried to put right the imbalance of his father's disordered desire by denying his own desires, but in tragic irony, he is unjustly accused and punished by his mother's rapist on the charge of raping his stepmother.

Of the play's three central characters, Hippolytus is the most complex. When we first meet him, he is offering sacrifices to Artemis and it's clear that he is indeed virginal and pious. But a servant identifies a chink in his supposed virtue. The servant praises Hippolytus for honoring Artemis, but asks him why he does not offer a sacrifice to Aphrodite.

> **Hippolytus:** I greet her from afar, for I am pure.
> **Servant:** Yet she's revered and famous among mortals.
> **Hippolytus:** I do not like a goddess worshiped at night.
> **Servant:** My son, to honor the gods is only just.
> **Hippolytus:** Men have their likes, in gods and men alike.
> **Servant:** I wish you fortune—and the good sense you need![8]

---

7. Euripides, *Hippolytus*, 1083.
8. Euripides, *Hippolytus*, 102-107.

To the Greek mind, piety is due to all the gods. Hippolytus may be chaste and pious toward Artemis, but he is arrogant and impious toward Aphrodite. Afraid for the young man, the servant prays to Aphrodite to spare Hippolytus in spite of his pride and folly, but he is too late. According to the terms of the play, her grievance against the young man is legitimate. He has failed in his duty to the goddess, and she wants vengeance.

But Hippolytus is also deficient in desire. As the play unfolds it becomes evident that his abstinence springs from disgust.

> *O Zeus, why have you settled women in the light of the sun, women, this bane mankind finds counterfeit? If you wished to propagate the human race, it was not from women that you should have given us this.*[9]

In the same speech he equates all women with Pandora, the woman created by the gods to punish men with lust and folly. He laments the "fatal necessity"[10] of marriage and rants that he "shall never take my fill of hating women... For they too are always in some way evil."[11] Hippolytus is not truly chaste; he is arrogant and unnatural. Chastity is a virtue acquired through humble submission to the sacramental goodness and decorum of sexual union. But to Hippolytus, women are punishment, and desire is death. In speaking of desire he shudders. "The very sound of such

---

9. Euripides, *Hippolytus*, 616-620.
10. Euripides, *Hippolytus*, 634.
11. Euripides, *Hippolytus*, 664, 666.

things makes me feel unclean."[12] Like Theseus and Phaedra, Hippolytus manifests grievous dissonance between duty and desire.

And ultimately it is disordered duty, not desire, that kills Hippolytus. He may be foolish and fastidious, but he is certainly innocent of the charge of rape—and yet he dies. In the final scene he is brought on stage in agony after a bull emerges from the sea and frightens his horses so that they bolt, dragging him through rocks and crags along the shore. This is Poseidon's answer to Theseus' prayer to kill his son. At this point Artemis appears in a belated deus ex machina to defend her acolyte and praise him for his devotion. She berates Theseus for his hasty prayer to Poseidon, who knew that Hippolytus was innocent but was bound by his promise to Theseus to curse his enemies. "The sea-lord, kindly disposed as he was towards you, granted what he had to grant seeing that he had made this promise."[13] Even the gods are bound by their vows, and Poseidon fulfills his duty, although it causes the death of the innocent. And so we see that in this play, along with countless other tragedies, the complex interweaving of disordered duty and desire catalyzes tragic action.

Many readers find sad stories more poignant or satisfying than comic ones. And in one sense they are more truthful in the way they contemplate the mysteries of the human condition, because sin and suffering are so mysterious to us. The proper response to the fall is lament and repen-

---

12. Euripides, *Hippolytus*, 655.
13. Euripides, *Hippolytus*, 1318-1319.

tance, and the enduring tragedies of the world invite us to both. I, too, find a strange consolation in a tragic narrative. Perhaps I feel that such stories can bear the weight of my personal grief and fragility, sometimes more than my lived experience that rightfully requires attention and care. When I am immersed in a tragic narrative, I release the burden of keeping-it-all-together and enter into Ajax's war trauma or Hamlet's dilemma or Anna Karenina's folly. This nourishes me by holding space for life's hardships and by awakening humane virtues such as compassion, humility, and discernment. Over many years of reading tragedy, I have often experienced the catharsis Aristotle describes. Tragedy provokes and purifies the pity and fear that builds over time in my frantic and anxious soul.

But what keeps tragedy from disintegrating into nihilism? Of all the cultures of the world, only now-defunct Western Christendom truly held a fundamental belief in the reality of a comic world. As we see in *Hippolytus*, Greek tragedies hold the tragic impulse at their core, as do many later literary tragedies such as Thomas Hardy's *Jude the Obscure* and Erich Marie Remarque's *All Quiet on the Western Front*. In these stories the world is implacable and chaotic, and the individual must stumble through the complexities of life as best he or she can in the face of impending doom. But even here such tragedies rarely descend to stark nihilism, because they are held by the tragic form. For the most part they still conform to Aristotle's proposed literary structure in *Poetics*. The plot must be internally cohesive with a clear beginning, middle, and end. The narrative must hold the audience's attention without being too long or too complex. It must contain elements such as a believable protagonist, a descent from prosperity to disaster, catastrophic reversals of fortune, and moments of recognition of fate or folly. In the case of pre-Christian and post-Christian tragedies, these formal and structural elements stand in for a meaningful world, creating a predictable narrative pattern that may not be comic but is nonetheless secure.

Furthermore, all of the great tragedies of the world depend upon an assumed cosmic moral order. Consider *Hippolytus*. Although the tragic action of the play is motivated by a merciless goddess, the sins of the characters are real, and they are punished. Even in cultures steeped in paganism or nihilism, the moral center of tragic narrative holds. The "right" people die for the "right" reasons. Thus the virtue at the heart of a true tragedy is justice.

Cosmic and human justice is far more evident in tragedies from the Christian era. Leo Tolstoy's *Anna Karenina* is like *Hippolytus* in that it explores the divided soul in matters of forbidden love, but in *Anna Karenina* justice is consistent rather than arbitrary. The tragic action results from choices made by the characters more than hardships inflicted upon them. These choices spring from the sins and sufferings of the divided soul.

Anna Karenina traces the trajectory of the eponymous heroine from aristocratic socialite to suicidal outcast in the wake of her affair with a dashing young officer. The structure of Anna's narrative follows the pattern of a classical tragedy in that Anna moves from the pinnacle of fortune to its nadir as a result of a tragic flaw. But what flaw? Is she not more sinned against than sinning—a winsome but vulnerable woman at the mercy of society's rigid double standards? Not according to Tolstoy, who illuminates the self-annihilation of the desire-driven lovers and the duty-driven cuckold. The novel takes us inside the interior worlds of Anna, her husband, Karenin, and her lover, Vronsky, exploring the division between duty and desire that destroys them all. Although Tolstoy presents Anna as extraordinarily appealing and censures the superficiality of aristocratic Russia, the novel frankly exposes the divided nature of the three central figures of the adulterous triangle, highlighting the fundamental truth that adultery harms rather than heals the divided soul.

Karenin is a man of duty. A wealthy and powerful Russian statesman, he is restrained, ambitious, and self-controlled. He eschews pleasure, orienting his time and energy toward vocational ambitions alone and denying himself affection and delight. Upon his marriage he gives his wife "all the feeling he was capable of,"[14] but is at best lukewarm. Wanting more, Anna rejects Karenin and unites herself with Vronsky, a man whose appetites define his relationships.

Vronsky is a rich, handsome young officer with a promising military career. Desire defines him. He takes what he wants, including Anna. "From the moment of Anna's love for him, he had considered his own right to her unassailable."[15] In Anna, Vronsky recognizes a soul whose desires and desirability outstrip his own.

Of course Anna is indeed immensely desirable. The ideal Russian socialite, she is beautiful, winsome, gracious, effer-

---

14. Tolstoy, *Anna Karenina*, 507.
15. Tolstoy, *Anna Karenina*, 305.

vescent—the undisputed darling of the aristocracy. At the beginning of the novel she inhabits a wide sphere of influence, but over the course of the story her world dwindles to a single object: Vronsky. "If I could be anything else but a mistress who passionately loves his caresses—but I cannot and do not want to be anything else."[16]

Having discarded her stifling marriage, Anna is cast into the giddy realms of desire unmitigated by duty. At first, this feels like freedom, but such a life precludes stabilizing bonds. Their only pledge is their passion, which proves feeble against encroaching pressures and insecurities. As their relationship deteriorates, Anna and Vronsky move to opposing poles of distorted desire. Vronsky, always more driven by physical appetites than Anna, attends aristocratic functions and social events, dissipating his frustrated energies. On the other hand, Anna demands more concentrated attention and increasingly extravagant declarations of love. "I'm not jealous, I'm dissatisfied," she stews. "My love grows ever more passionate and self-centered, and his keeps fading and fading."[17] Soon Anna is so consumed by her desire to be desired that she utterly rejects Vronsky's declaration that he will stay out of a sense of duty. "If he is kind and gentle towards me out of duty, without loving me, and I am not to have what I want—that is a thousand times worse even than anger! It's hell!"[18] Their once-swollen mutual desire collapses inward, and they drain one another like two orbiting black holes.

---

16. Tolstoy, *Anna Karenina*, 763.
17. ibid
18. ibid

Meanwhile, duty-driven Karenin is in a similar state of disintegration. When he first discovers his wife's affair, he coldly permits it, granting her "the rights of an honest wife, without fulfilling her duties" as long as "my name is not disgraced."[19] Later he refuses a divorce on religious grounds. In spite of his attempt at moral superiority, however, he is in agony. But he denies himself the humanizing experience of mourning. Instead of grieving, he effectively amputates the desiring part of his soul, cutting himself off from giving and receiving mercy and love, and he nurses his bitterness and misery for the rest of his life.

In the end, Anna's narrative culminates in bleak but cohesive justice. By denying either duty or desire, all three members of the doomed love triangle wound their own souls unto death, either literally or metaphorically. The novel portrays a stark microcosm of the divided cosmos played out in the fractured world of one tragic marriage. But at a fundamental level, the tragic impulse does not ultimately triumph. Rather, it is justice that triumphs. The novel acknowledges that the sins of our divided souls breed disorder and division; they cry out to be healed or to be avenged. Deep down we intrinsically recognize that duty and desire belong together. Tragedy tells us what happens when we remain divided.

At the heart of tragic justice is an ancient and powerful image: the wheel. Cosmology dating as far back as the Babylonian empire imagines the cosmos as a revolving circle. The celestial rotation of the stars governs the affairs of men, whose fortunes rise and fall. The Greeks embodied

---

19. Tolstoy, *Anna Karenina*, 320.

this concept in a goddess, Tyche, which became the Roman goddess, Fortuna, always depicted holding a wheel. *Rota fortuna*, Fortune's Wheel, became emblematic of the pagan belief in arbitrary fate. The gods were capricious and life was unpredictable, thus the goddess spins the wheel at random, dispensing to some misery and to others prosperity. Nobody really knew whether the whims of fortune were due to chance or the gods, but the results were the same. This version of the wheel is embedded in Greek tragedies like *Hippolytus*.

As the pagan world gave way to Christendom, the image of the wheel remained, but in a new form. In his famous treatise on suffering, *The Consolation of Philosophy*, Boethius straddles the pagan and the Christian world with a new conception of Fortune's Wheel. Born in the late fifth-century AD, Boethius was both a Roman and a Christian. In Consolation, he distinguishes between fate and providence. Like the pagans, he acknowledges the cyclical nature of fate, but he argues that a benevolent providence ultimately provides purpose to suffering and converges toward an ultimate good. In other words, he posits that Fortune's Wheel is not ultimately tragic, but comic. Boethius' ideas mark a watershed transition from pagan to medieval thought.

It is nearly impossible to overstate the influence of Boethius on the Western mind. The medievals loved Fortune's Wheel. The image is ubiquitous in the Middle Ages, saturating both sacred and secular art, as well as literature, philosophy, scholasticism and even colloquialisms. Throw a stone in medieval research, and you will hit the Wheel.

The difference between the pagan wheel and the medieval wheel is profound. The medieval *rota fortuna*, like the cosmos itself, turns not by chance but by providence. The fates of nations and individuals rise and fall, governed by divine will toward an ultimate end. It may *feel* arbitrary, but it is actually meaningful. Hamlet was right to muse, "There is special providence in the fall of a sparrow."[20] This is the version of the wheel at the core of the greatest and most enduring tragedies. When Anna flings herself under the train or the curtain drops on Hamlet's corpse, we grieve, but we sense that the center will hold and the wheel will turn, this time upwards.

Tragedy is part and parcel of a comic world. It explores the divided soul through the lens of justice. But it is incomplete. Justice is the governing virtue of the tragic sphere, but in reality justice never stands alone. Mercy is the missing piece of tragedy. Without mercy, the tragic impulse reigns. Perhaps this is why Shakespeare puts his transcendent speech on mercy in one of his comedies.

> *The quality of mercy is not strained;*
> *It droppeth as the gentle rain from heaven*
> *Upon the place beneath. It is twice blest;*
> *It blesseth him that gives and him that takes:*
> *'T is mightiest in the mightiest; it becomes*
> *The thronèd monarch better than his crown:*
> *His scepter shows the force of temporal power,*
> *The attribute to awe and majesty,*
> *Wherein doth sit the dread and fear of kings;*
> *But mercy is above this sceptred sway;*

---

20. Shakespeare, *Hamlet*, 5.2.157.

It is enthronèd in the hearts of kings,
It is an attribute to God himself;
And earthly power doth then show likest God's
When mercy seasons justice. Therefore, Jew,
Though justice be thy plea, consider this,
That, in the course of justice, none of us
Should see salvation: we do pray for mercy;
And that same prayer doth teach us all to render
The deeds of mercy. I have spoke thus much
To mitigate the justice of thy plea.[21]

I often wonder what my life would have been if justice had been unmitigated by mercy. Looking back, I gratefully identify just consequences of my moral failures, but I also see decisive moments when grace kept me from falling. I am not luckier or more beloved than anybody else; it is simply that God is conspiring to save me, and He does the same for everybody who will receive it. By His light, I see light; by His mercy, I see mercy. Jesus interrupts the tragic fall of the whole world and transfigures all things by grace. And mercy does not suspend justice; it completes it. Based on my early childhood, my whole life should have been a tragedy—and it almost was—but Christ placed Himself between me and a stage littered with corpses.

He did the same for my mother, tormented as she was throughout her life. I was with her when she fell asleep for the last time. She took her last struggling breath in the witching hours of a sultry spring night in a Phoenix hospital room. I remember how it fell over me like a gentle rain that

---

21. Shakespeare, *The Merchant of Venice*, 4.1.179–198.

she was no longer suffering. I had never known her happy, but there she was, beyond the veil, beholding Christ in joy. Right now she is in paradise, healed and whole, while I am still a divided soul. God is merciful, and He answered my prayers for the mother I need, although I do not know her that way yet. Her life and legacy was destined for a happy ending. So is mine, and so is yours. The tragic impulse does not triumph, because "mercy triumphs over judgment."[22] When we know this we can truly say glory to God for all things.

---

22. James 2:13 (KJV).

6

THE KING AND THE MAN

The Drama of Succession

One night when my son was nine years old, I came upon him sitting cross-legged on his bed with the *Odyssey* propped open on his lap. He was reading about Telemachus, whose father—the great Odysseus—sailed away to war twenty years ago when the young man was only a baby. Telemachus' only connection to his noble father was through the place he lived and the stories he knew. Now he is almost grown and longs to become a king and a man like his father, but he does not know how.

I watched my own son reading until he looked up at me and said in his thoughtful way, "Mama, Telemachus just asked Athena, 'does any man ever really know his father?'"[1] He paused. "Do you think that's true?" I told him that I didn't know.

In 1973 literary critic Harold Bloom published *The Anxiety of Influence: A Theory on Poetry* in which he argues that generations of authors are locked in a psychological

---

1. Paraphrased from Homer, *The Odyssey*, trans. Robert Fagles, 1.250.

struggle to assimilate and cast off the influences of their literary forebears. Emerging writers are like Telemachus, left behind while his father triumphs in a glorious battle beyond his reach, his only guide the brilliance of past reputations. To Bloom, living authors are the sons who never really know their fathers. Only writers who overcome the anxiety of influence to forge their own creative paths, he claims, will go on to craft enduring literature. In many ways Bloom's conclusions are themselves predictable and even banal derivatives of modernity, but his theory is nonetheless compelling in so far as it acknowledges how vulnerable it feels to pass anything valuable from one generation to the next.

When my mother died she left me an heirloom set of beautiful French fine bone china from 1870. I represent the fifth generation of women in my family to serve Christmas dinner on the delicate green-and-gilt dishes. They are perhaps the most precious things I own. When I unwrapped it all, dish by dish, in the weeks after her death, I found one broken plate. I held the pieces in my hands and wept; something lovely and priceless had been damaged on my watch. The truth is that we are responsible for so many precious things, whether antique china, poetry, children, or our own divided souls, and we long to be worthy of what is entrusted to us.

The anxiety of influence highlights a personal as well as a creative paradox: we become who we are because of our forebears, but we cannot become who we are without separating ourselves from them. Bloom is probably right that authors experience anxiety of influence—and so does everybody else. If fathers represent the formative influences of the past, we experience this vulnerability not only with our parents, but in many contexts—political, educational, ideological, relational, communal, and spiritual. We are haunted by fear and hope about past and future generations. Like Telemachus, we may not know our fathers, but we are responsible for what they left behind.

Because the problem of anxiety of influence is universally human, literature wrestles with it in multitudinous ways, particularly in relation to the conflicts between duty and desire. Shakespeare's *Henry IV, Part 1* explicitly explores the anxiety of influence in the divided soul.

King Henry IV sits on the throne of England, but his reign is insecure. Only two years before the play begins, Henry seized the throne from his cousin, the weak and frivolous King Richard II. Henry is a shrewder, cannier, more capable ruler, but he is a usurper. All of England waits to see what will happen to the new monarch and his realm in the wake of his divisive rise, including many enemies who are ready to pounce. Among them are Lord Northumberland and his son, Henry Percy, who initially supported Henry's claim but soon reveal themselves to be as treacherous to Henry as they were to Richard. In Act I Henry receives news that they have joined forces with the Welsh to overthrow him and place yet another usurper on the throne in his stead. Under the shadow of this burgeoning crisis, Henry must respond to protect his throne.

Yet the play does not open with the impending civil war, but with another kind of conflict. Before Henry learns of Northumberland's defection, he praises him in court for valiant deeds accomplished alongside his son, the young knight, Henry Percy. His words reveal the underlying conflict of the play, which is not only political, but domestic—and ultimately existential.

The king's problem is his son, who is nothing like Northumberland's son, for which he expresses bitter disappointment.

> *Yea, there thou mak'st me sad, and mak'st me sin*
> *In envy that my Lord Northumberland*
> *Should be the father to so blest a son,*
> *A son who is the theme of Honor's tongue,*
> *Amongst a grove the very straightest plant,*
> *Who is sweet Fortune's minion and her pride;*
> *Whilst I, by looking on the praise of him,*
> *See riot and dishonor stain the brow*
> *Of my young Harry. O, that it could be proved*
> *That some night-tripping fairy had exchanged*
> *In cradle-clothes our children where they lay,*
> *And called mine "Percy," his "Plantagenet"!*
> *Then would I have his Harry, and he mine.*[2]

The king bemoans that Northumberland's son has achieved victory and honor alongside his father, while his own son—also named Henry—has so far only achieved only "riot and dishonor." He even wishes his own son away, longing to replace him with Henry Percy.

The two young men share a name, but both are called something else in the play. Prince Henry is most often called

---

2. Shakespeare, *Henry IV, Part 1*, 1.1.77–89.

The King and the Man

Hal, a childish nickname more suited to a peasant than to the heir to the throne. On the other hand, Henry Percy is called Hotspur, implying knightly zeal and skill. In a literary sense, the young Henries are inverted doubles of one another. They share a name, but both are known by nicknames that mask their true identities behind widespread perceptions—particularly those of King Henry. Is Prince Hal as riotous and dishonorable as his father believes? Is Hotspur as admirable and honorable as the king envisions? Is reputation an indicator of true identity?

King Henry's speech stirs deep waters. If sons do not truly know their fathers, isn't it possible that fathers do not truly know their sons? And if that is the case, what impact does that have on everybody involved? The questions are searingly relevant, because so many of us have been damaged by rifts between generations. In the play the issue is complicated by the circumstances of King Henry's reign. Because he is a usurper, his legacy is uncertain. Does not justice demand a reckoning? Is Northumberland's rebellion divine retribution or political treachery? The sins of the father always besiege his sons. Either way what Henry needs is help—and the most essential help of all is the promise of a strong successor. But young Hal does not seem to fit the bill.

Human history is haunted by problems of succession. Who will care for the legacy of the past in the city and the soul? The burden is heavy. The specter of disrupted succession has resulted in countless sins and sufferings over thousands of years, undergirding practices like polygamy, primogeniture, and the trafficking of child brides. It motivated Henry VIII, Napoleon, and so many others to discard their wives. In Shakespeare's day it plagued Queen Elizabeth. The personal and political cost of the problems and pressures of succession throughout generations of human existence is incalculable, and this play demonstrates the gravity of the universal dilemma.

It seems to me that the problem of succession is at the root of the anxiety of influence. In Plato's *Republic*, the great philosopher Socrates asserts that the city is like the soul and that we ought to rule both by the same virtues, avoiding the same vices. The implications of this are profound. If Socrates is right, a healthy king will rightly govern himself and his land. By extension, however, a divided king further divides his realm. And since the character of the father transmits to the son and the character of the king to his land, we know that everybody will leave a legacy. Fathers bear the burden of passing on a legacy; sons bear the burden of receiving it. If fathers represent the past and sons the present, we have an immense web of complex dilemmas on the personal, public, and historical levels. And this is as fraught for us as it is for Henry and Hal.

The problem of succession is foremost on King Henry's mind as he confronts Northumberland's rebellion. If young Hal was a stronger successor, the kingdom would be more stable and a successful revolt less likely. So when King Henry bewails his prodigal son, he speaks not only as a man and a father, but as the king, raising fundamental questions about identity that impact not just his family but the future of the kingdom itself. But who *is* Henry? A king is both a position and a person—duty and desire—and, in this instance, both are dubious. Henry was not born to be king; he seized the throne, and under questionable circumstances at that. Nonetheless, he is a crowned king in need of support from his son. At the same time he is also a disappointed father with a rebellious son. Where does the king leave off and the man begin? What is he to do about the ambiguity of his actions as both king and man, especially now that war is brewing? The questions are myriad; the stakes are high. And the nexus of all this complexity is young Hal.

We meet Hal immediately after his father's speech. The scene shifts abruptly from the king's court to the Boar's Head Inn, a disreputable London tavern where Hal and his companion, Sir John Falstaff, stumble onstage after a bout of drinking. Falstaff is old, fat, and debauched—no fit companion for any impressionable young man, let alone the heir to the throne. But he is also witty, jolly, and delightfully good fun. Unlike King Henry, Falstaff rejoices in his connection with Hal. Where the king is guarded and punitive, Falstaff is merry and expansive. Together Falstaff and Hal carouse the streets of London.

The central conflict of the play is the war between these two competing influences in Prince Hal's life. King Henry invokes duty and Falstaff desire, and in these first two scenes we see the existential conflict of opposing forces on the soul of the young. All three of them are burdened by the staggering implications of Hal's free will. If he neglects his father, they may lose the throne and their lives. But even that duty is unclear, because King Henry ascended to the throne by betraying the rightful king. How much has that motivated Hal's withdrawal from court? On the other hand, if Hal casts off Falstaff, is he not casting off his only true friend? Does he not jettison any hope of meaningful freedom by adhering to the king's machiavellian legacy?

Both of the older men are father figures to young Hal, but neither is a whole person. Together they represent the fragments of the divided soul. Shakespeare wrote about many kings, but King Henry IV is the only one who lacks a clear dramatic locus of identity. Every other important Shakespearean king has at least one soliloquy—a speech delivered alone onstage that reveals the character's true motives. Audiences can trust soliloquies because the character on stage is not speaking to deceive. They are intimate, revealing moments between the character and the audience. Through their soliloquies we know that Richard III and Macbeth are wicked while Henry VI (a different Henry) and Hamlet are noble. But in all three of his plays, our King Henry never once speaks alone onstage. His identity is the image he projects; the king has swallowed the man. There are certainly moments where he is sincere, but without a soliloquy we cannot be sure. And he expects the same implacable restraint from Hal. King Henry demands duty but denies desire.

It is no wonder, then, that Hal is drawn to Falstaff, that man of appetites. Falstaff denies himself nothing, and he urges the prince to share in his indulgences. Their banter is for the most part charming, and they enjoy much light-hearted revelry, but all is not carefree between them. Throughout the first half of the play we see them in only two settings: the sordid Boars Head Inn where they are surrounded by drunks and whores, and a hillside where they commit highway robbery for a purse of gold to squander on a wild night. And even that is an illusion—Hal faked the robbery to play a practical joke on Falstaff. Although it is real, the bond between them is vulgar and unsettling. Many times they speak to one another as though living on borrowed time, most poignantly and famously when Falstaff pleads with Hal not to reject him after Hal ascends the throne.

> *No, my good lord, banish Peto, banish Bardolph, banish Poins, but for sweet Jack Falstaff, kind Jack Falstaff, true Jack Falstaff, valiant Jack Falstaff, and therefore more valiant being as he is old Jack Falstaff, banish not him thy Harry's company, banish not him thy Harry's company. Banish plump Jack, and banish all the world.*[3]

That final sentence reveals the essence of their bond—Falstaff offers Hal not the narrow constraints of a stolen throne, but "all the world." Yet the world is not all it's cracked up to be. Devoid of duty, Falstaff represents the glut of unrestrained desire.

To become his true self, Hal must reconcile within himself the opposition between distorted duty and desire as represented by these two competing father figures. Only then will he be worthy of a legitimate crown. In order to become the man and king he is meant to be, Hal must shake off the anxiety of influence that plagues his divided soul. He

---

3. Shakespeare, *Henry IV, Part 1*, 1.2.432-438.

will forge his true identity not by avoiding the problems of succession, but by assuming its mantle as *himself* instead of as a projection of who King Henry and Falstaff want him to be. When that happens, the land—and his soul—will finally be at peace, for only a healed king can heal his realm.

I love this play because it is a microcosm of the human condition. Like Hal, we are tempted to poles of rigid self-denial and indulgent passion. Some of us migrate toward one extreme or the other, while others vacillate wildly between them. Both are joyless, truncated states of existence. Few of us will govern anything like a land, but all of us are called to rightly govern ourselves, and none of us can rule the realm of our own souls without reckoning with our inherited internal division. We are the sons who do not know our fathers but long to be worthy of our inheritance. We are also the sons haunted by the sins (and sometimes even the glories) of our fathers, and we long to exorcize the ghosts. But how do we come to terms with the past? How can Hal cast off the anxiety of Henry and Falstaff's influence and become worthy of his rightful crown?

Act 3 of every Shakespeare play contains a turning point—a hinge that turns the action of the play toward its proper end. And in two essential moments in Act 3, Hal takes action to reconcile the opposing forces of distorted duty and desire in his life. Hal models how to unify a soul on the psychological level. King Henry summons Hal to court to rebuke his prodigality and recruit his aid. The painful conversation which follows takes place in court, King Henry seated on his throne with Hal standing alone before him. The king upbraids Hal for his shameful associations, dissipated conduct, absence from court, and carelessness with the royal reputation. He pulls no punches.

> *Thy place in council thou hast rudely lost,*
> *Which by thy younger brother is supplied,*
> *And art almost an alien to the hearts*
> *Of all the court and princes of my blood.*
> *The hope and expectation of thy time*
> *Is ruined, and the soul of every man*
> *Prophetically do forethink thy fall.*[4]

Thus chastised, Hal excuses and explains himself, but the king does not relent. Hal's apologies smack of pretense, and the king will have none of it. But at the height of the argument, something changes. The king weeps. Henry's tears are significant enough in themselves—until this point we've seen no vulnerability in the king. But it is the words he utters before the tears that lend an even deeper sorrow to the moment.

> *For thou hast lost thy princely privilege*
> *With vile participation. Not an eye*
> *But is aweary of thy common sight,*
> *Save mine, which hath desired to see thee more,*
> *Which now doth that I would not have it do, Make blind itself*
> *with foolish tenderness.*[5]

King Henry weeps because he has lost his son to Falstaff. Hal's "vile participation" with the fat knight has made every-

---
4. Shakespeare, *Henry IV, Part 1*, 3.2.32-38
5. Shakespeare, *Henry IV, Part 1*, 3.2.86-91.

body sick of the sight of him—everybody but his father, who "hath desired to see [him] more." Some interpret Henry's tears as calculated, some as sincere. Either way, they are the turning point. Hal ceases justifying himself and utters the promise that is the crux of the play: "I shall hereafter, my thrice gracious lord, be more myself."[6]

Isn't this everything? Until now, Hal displaces responsibility for his actions on external forces. But meaningful healing first requires humility and repentance. Regardless of the valid excuses and explanations, and regardless of the undeniable fact that Hal's critical and withholding father was himself responsible for much of the young man's damaged soul, Hal will only overcome the past by reckoning with himself. The experience is painful, but Hal does not withdraw in shame; he responds with conviction. Hal's authentic selfhood emerges in light of kingly rebuke and fatherly tears. Notice that he does not respond that he shall hereafter be more compliant, docile, or obedient. He does not vow to conform to his father's expectations. Instead he declares his intention to inhabit his true identity. This implies both a recognition that his recent actions conflict with his true nature and a realization of what must be done to recover himself.

From this point, Hal is a new man. Henry's rebuke recalls him to his duty. Hal is no longer Hal—he is now Henry of Monmouth, Prince of Wales, and his family and his future throne are under attack. Suddenly he has a part to play in something beyond himself. He is not just a man; he is also a future king who is prepared to cast off self-indulgence and

---

6. Shakespeare, *Henry IV, Part 1*, 3.2.92-93.

take up the mantle of succession. In resolving to be "more myself," Hal also acquires the nature of a king.

But there is more. In the same scene Hal and his father begin to strategize their response to the Welsh rebellion, a conversation in which the political and personal overlap as Hal engages his father as an equal for the first time. This creates conflict within the strong-willed king, who responds by comparing Hal to Richard II and Hotspur to himself. When Henry usurped the throne, he was a rebel like Hotspur, and Richard was on the defensive as Hal is now. Henry sinks into ambiguity again, praising Hotspur's "never dying-honor"[7] while wondering if Hal will "fight against [him] under Percy's pay."[8]

Once again, Henry the king, haunted by his own history, shrouds Henry the man. But Hal stands firm.

Do not think so. You shall not find it so…
I will redeem all this on Percy's head,
And, in the closing of some glorious day,
Be bold to tell you that I am your son.[9]

His father's comparisons and accusations do not shake Hal's resolve to henceforth fulfill his duty to father and realm, but he refuses to identify himself merely by his role. He responds to his father's unfair accusation by referring to himself not as heir, but as "your son." Hal unites responsibility with relationship. He will not reduce himself to king;

---

7. Shakespeare, *Henry IV, Part 1*, 3.2.106.
8. Shakespeare, *Henry IV, Part 1*, 3.2.126.
9. Shakespeare, *Henry IV, Part 1*, 3.2.129-134.

he will also remain a man.

But what about Falstaff? What will the young prince do about his bawdy companion now that he is reconciled to his duty as the prince? After speaking with his father, Hal returns to the Boar's Head Inn where he finds Falstaff trying to swindle the hostess out of the bill. They negotiate the debt, and the dialogue is riddled with subtext. Falstaff knows that the king summoned Hal to account, and he senses an impending change. Although the tone is lighthearted, the conversation begins to mirror Hal's encounter with King Henry in that Falstaff demands allegiance to the terms of their relationship—in this case, rank desire rather than duty.

> **Hostess:** *So he doth you, my lord, and said this other day you owed him a thousand pound.*
> **Hal:** *Sirrah, do I owe you a thousand pound?*
> **Falstaff:** *A thousand pound, Hal? A million. Thy love is worth a million; thou owest me thy love.*[10]

Underneath their banter runs an undercurrent of poignant appeal. Falstaff is not merely begging for money; he is pleading to maintain their relationship. Yes, their mutual indulgence of unbridled appetite is disordered, but the deeper desire for love is sincere. Most moving of all are Falstaff's continual references to the problem of Hal's succession.

---

10. Shakespeare, *Henry IV, Part 1*, 3.3.123-126.

Hal: *Darest thou be as good as thy word now?*
Falstaff: *Why, Hal, thou knowest, as thou art but man, I dare, but as thou art prince, I fear thee as I fear the roaring of the lion's whelp.*[11]

If Henry wants Hal to become fully a king, Falstaff wants him to remain only a man. But Hal maintains his commitment to unity. He rages at Falstaff for trying to filch on his debt. "But, sirrah, there's no room for faith, truth, nor honesty in this bosom of thine . . . Art thou not ashamed?"[12] In this rebuke Hal demonstrates genuine love for Falstaff, calling him to shed his dishonorable habits and become worthy of trust. But Hal doesn't stop with reproof; he offers Falstaff a real chance to redeem himself by procuring for him a command in his infantry.

> *Jack, meet me tomorrow in the Temple hall*
> *At two o'clock in the afternoon;*
> *There shalt thou know thy charge, and there receive*
> *Money and order for their furniture.*
> *The land is burning. Percy stands on high,*
> *And either we or they must lower lie.*[13]

For the first time he speaks to Falstaff as king as well as companion, inviting him to transcend his former self and be his partner in both duty and desire. These two transformative conversations reflect Hal's existential struggle

---

11. Shakespeare, *Henry IV, Part 1*, 3.3.134-136.
12. Shakespeare, *Henry IV, Part 1*, 3.3.142-143, 150.
13. Shakespeare, *Henry IV, Part 1*, 3.3.183-188.

to overcome the opposition between disordered duty and desire. We, too, are strained to the breaking point between competing forces, but Hal shows us how to wrestle through the inherited anxiety of influence to unify our divided souls. Upon recognizing the rupture within himself, Hal changes, casting off the destructive influence of his disordered fathers. But although he recognizes their limitations, in this play Hal rejects neither his father nor his friend. Instead, he gleans from them while preserving the integrity of his newfound identity. Rejecting the bad, he assimilates the good. This too is an example for us. To be worthy to rule the kingdom of ourselves, we pursue unity between duty and desire, choosing to be both responsible and relational, virtuous and vivacious, public and personal. Like Hal, we must harmonize the dutiful king and the desirous man within us.

The second half of the play continues to trace Hal's trajectory of growth. Significantly, as Hal rises, Hotspur sinks, gradually unmasked as reckless, arrogant, and insolent. Hotspur's reputation as an honorable knight is debunked; it turns out that reputation is not a true indicator of identity. And Hal's next order of business is to rid the land of Hotspur—that living but unworthy embodiment of his father's expectations, disappointments, and mistakes. When they meet in battle, Hal expresses his intent to expunge his foe:

> *Two stars keep not their motion in one sphere,*
> *Nor can one England brook a double reign*

Of Harry Percy and the Prince of Wales.[14]

Hotspur is Hal's shadow self, the specter of the past and obstacle to his future. In order to overcome his personal anxiety of influence once and for all, Hal must defeat his rival. Soon Hotspur lies slain by the prince's sword, but Hal disclaims public recognition of his victory, further evidence of his intact sense of self. For Hal it is enough that his rival is removed and the kingdom is secure.

But does Hal's hard-fought unity of soul extend beyond himself to heal the contending fathers who laid such heavy burdens on him? In one sense, yes, in another, no. In the final battle, Hal directly saves his father's life from a traitorous enemy, and he indirectly saves Falstaff by giving him credit for Hotspur's death even after the knight dishonorably flees from battle. Although they have done him wrong, Hal reconciles with both, demanding neither penance nor amendment. He accepts them as they are—something they never did for him. Prince Hal teaches us that the transfiguring legacy of a unified soul is forgiveness.

Henry IV, Part 1 teaches us how to pursue peace with the past. Parents give life and legacy to their children; children preserve the life and legacy of their parents. This is true for better and for worse within families and societies. We all must reckon with the "fathers" in our lives. Harold Bloom believes this is a creative movement, but it seems to me that it is a spiritual one. The anxiety of influence is no doubt real, but it is purposeful, meant to be a crucible of

---

14. Shakespeare, *Henry IV, Part 1*, 5.4.64-66.

grace for the reunification of the divided soul. This is all the more beautiful to me because ultimately neither Henry nor Falstaff change. Falstaff remains a coward and a weakling, and King Henry ends the play issuing executive orders to protect his stolen throne. But Hal chooses a different way.

Like Hal, we dwell in a polarity not of our own making. We have inherited the divided soul, which is not our fault, but it is our responsibility. Distorted duty and desire tempt us every day, but we are not doomed to eternal division, no matter what influences surround us. Ultimately our lives converge not toward separation, but *union* with the Father. All of our dissonance will one day resolve into divine harmony when we enter into eternal communion with God. Our earthly fathers fail, but our Heavenly Father does not. Hal shows us how to take honorable and unifying action on this side of the veil of eternity, but in the end our divided souls will be healed not by our own efforts but by the love of the perfect Father. Ultimately, as Julian of Norwich wrote, "sin is necessary, but all shall be well, and shall be well, and all manner of things shall be well."[15]

---

15. Julian of Norwich, *The Revelation of Divine Love in Sixteen Showings Made to Dame Julian of Norwich*, 102.

7

ELINOR DASHWOOD IN SEARCH OF THE HOLY GRAIL

Desire Submerged in Duty

"The happy person both lives well and acts well. Happiness, therefore, is the best, noblest, and most complete thing."
—Aristotle

Today was a full day. I woke up at 5:30am to write, taught a series of classes on Homer, Plato, and Dante, met with the headmistress of our school, dropped my daughter off at dance, ate dinner in the car while listening to an audiobook for a podcast tomorrow, drove to my son's basketball game, left early to fetch my daughter from dance, attended an informational meeting about how I can support her competition dance team, stopped for groceries on the way home, walked in the door to put away the groceries, feed the dogs, unload the dishwasher, switch over the laundry, and, at last, sat down once more to write.

I dislike the pace. Every day I fantasize about a cottage we lived in long ago in Whitby, England. Perched on the cliffs overlooking the North Sea, it is plastered in white and shingled in gray. A circular reading room outfitted with a writing desk and a squashy armchair, lined with a curve of mullioned windows, looks out over the sea. At night we would throw open the windows and fall asleep to the lulling of waves and crooning of sea birds. I remember long rambles back and forth to the shore, little Jack and Lucy lugging their buckets and spades to construct sandcastles and collect sea snails. If the chilly north wind picked up, we warmed ourselves with creamy Yorkshire tea and sauntered back to the cottage to read *Peter Rabbit* or *The Wind in the Willows*. In Whitby I walked back and forth to the market every day, and I hung the laundry out to dry in the salty breeze on clear days. Our clothes always smelled like the sea.

My English idyll is a sharp contrast to these current staccato days. As I press forward, I often set my teeth and pray, "These are the years. These are the years. Lord Jesus Christ, have mercy on me, a sinner." But although I imagine a simpler life, what parts of it would I give up? Nothing. My work is fruitful, my community is rich and varied, my home is my domain, and my family is the most important work of all. And so I am striving to be faithful with the life I have been given. In this I know that I am not alone. Everybody I know struggles under the weight of the frantic pace of modern life; we are all wrestling not only with cosmic, existential questions, but also with the ordinary, mundane conflicts between duty and desire.

The stories that acknowledge this dilemma are myriad because the problem is universal. In a world where duty and desire are at variance, all of us live and labor in disharmony, a truth which the Bible acknowledges frankly when God speaks to Adam and Eve of the fruit of their sin. To Eve He says: "I will greatly multiply thy sorrow and thy conception; in sorrow thou shalt bring forth children; and thy

desire shall be to thy husband, and he shall rule over thee."[1]
He also speaks to Adam:

> *Cursed is the ground for thy sake; in sorrow shalt thou eat of it all the days of thy life; Thorns also and thistles shall it bring forth to thee; and thou shalt eat the herb of the field; In the sweat of thy face shalt thou eat bread, till thou return unto the ground.*[2]

The breach between duty and desire robs work of delight. No longer does Eve revel in life-giving, nor does Adam rejoice in labor. I often wonder what Adam thought and felt as he planted and hoed and weeded and gathered his scant harvests outside of Eden; what Eve experienced after giving birth in pain and rocking her little sons to sleep in a new and frightening world. We, too, are exiled from paradise, recognizing that we should exult in our work, but in reality often collapsing under its burden.

It seems to me that duty is the guiding principle of meaningful work, but desire ennobles and elevates the task toward a purposeful end. Rarely do I begin routine tasks because I enjoy them, but such tasks are often transfigured by their purpose. Examples abound, from emails to exercise to eating vegetables. I schedule appointments and labor over lesson plans because I want to accomplish useful work in the world. I walk miles a day and eat brown rice and vegetables because I want to be healthy into old age. I cheer at my son's basketball games and volunteer at

---

1. Genesis 3:16 (KJV).
2. Genesis 3:17-18 (KJV).

my daughter's dance studio because I want to dignify them in their pursuits. The desire for an expected good extends beyond the task into the transcendent—otherwise it feels like mere drudgery. Humans need to know that the mundane is meaningful.

This principle is also at the core of stories with higher stakes than these everyday events. According to this ethic, characters must temporarily sublimate their desires to a higher duty leading to a sure reward. This pattern is grounded in the same eternal comic impulse we've examined before. In this chapter we will look at two iconic characters who embody it—Sir Galahad and Elinor Dashwood, both heroic individuals who submerge desire in duty, suffering and sacrificing along the way until the story eventually culminates in a triumphant conclusion.

Quest narratives populate the canons of literature from texts including everything from the book of Exodus to the *Aeneid* to *The Lord of the Rings*. Tolkien himself was a medieval scholar who drew liberally from the Arthurian legend, an exceedingly rich constellation of medieval stories that have influenced virtually all Western writers of heroic tales since their inception in the early Middle Ages. The legend of King Arthur is not a single, unified narrative, but a collection of loosely-connected stories from a wide variety of sources ranging across Europe from the fifth to the fifteenth centuries. Wildly popular from their earliest days, they are also proto-narratives for a host of later stories, including the Star Wars franchise, Shakespeare's *Romeo and Juliet,* and the gunslinger archetype of the American West.

The most famous quest in the Arthurian canon is, of

course, the search for the Holy Grail, the cup from which Christ drank at the Last Supper when He instituted the sacrament of communion. No object more sacred to Christian tradition can be imagined, (except perhaps the remnants of the holy cross, which indeed has its own long and storied history) and, throughout the tales, the best and bravest of Arthur's knights take up the quest to find it. None are worthy, however, and all fail, until Galahad arrives at Camelot during the feast of Pentecost. When he approaches the Round Table, he is led to the Siege Perilous, the vacant seat reserved for the knight destined to find the Holy Grail. Even to approach the enchanted seat is an act of valor—everybody knows that unworthy knights fall down dead if they presume. But Galahad sits and is unscathed. This, they all realize, is the greatest of all knights, worthy even to grasp the Holy Grail.

Sir Galahad is already noteworthy in Camelot as the only knight to ever beat the peerless Sir Lancelot in a fair fight, a significant event because Lancelot just happens to be his father. The quintessential knight, Sir Lancelot embodies the spirit of the Middle Ages. In him converge multiple streams of medieval literary and cultural conventions, including the code of chivalry and the tradition of courtly love. But he is complicated. His courage and skill are unequaled, but he is often rash and foolish, entangling himself in double binds. For example, his notorious affair with Queen Guinevere is complicated by the principles of courtly love, which compel a knight to pine for a lady and a lady to reward a favored knight in turn, regardless of marital status. In the strange but very real logic of courtly love, since Lancelot is the greatest of knights, he *ought* to love the highest of ladies, and she him. On the other hand, he also owes his full allegiance to the king, which of course includes, well, not sleeping with his wife. This is only one example of the complex web of social and moral dilemmas that are woven into the Lancelot legends.

Galahad's birth reflects the ambiguity of his father. Lancelot loves Queen Guinevere, so he will not take another woman to bed, but King Pelles, whose job it is to guard the Holy Grail, prophecies that his daughter, Elaine, and Lancelot are destined to conceive the knight who will find the grail. With this knowledge, Pelles gives Elaine a magic ring that allows her to transform her appearance. She uses it to take Guinevere's form and dupe Lancelot into conceiving Galahad. After his birth, the baby is raised in a convent until he grows into manhood and emerges to fulfill his destiny.

Galahad, unlike his father, is a paragon of Christian virtue, unsullied by the divided soul of his age. Medieval scholars often cast him as a literary analogue to the historical Knights Templar—the famous monk-knights. Soon after becoming a knight, Galahad challenges his father to a joust as befits a young knight trying to prove his mettle. At first Lancelot, who has never been beaten, sneers, but Galahad easily unseats him and his triumph symbolizes the conquest of holiness over worldlines. But it also functions on a psychological level—the young knight overcomes the anxiety of Lancelot's influence before joining the Round Table.

Having proved his worth, Galahad sets out in search for the grail. Along the way, he overcomes trials and temptations with knightly virtues—courage, chastity, piety, honor, zeal. Many situations test his dutiful soul, but Galahad always does the right thing. Like many medieval heroes, he is not a flawed human character, but an idealized embodiment of prescribed virtues. Galahad demonstrates that duty guides a hero on his quest.

But Galahad is no stoic; virtue alone is not his reward. After many ordeals, he arrives at Corbenic Castle—the home of his grandfather King Pelles—along with two worthy companions, Sir Pervival and Sir Bors, where they discover the grail hidden in a secret room. All three knights are ushered into the presence of the grail, but Percival and Bors are struck blind by its sacred light. Only Galahad can withstand its glory. King Pelles thus entrusts the grail to the worthy knight, who removes it to a holy place. One morning Galahad encounters the grail suspended in midair surrounded by a host of angels singing. Rejoicing in his prize, Galahad embraces his companions and commends them to God. After kneeling in prayer, he ascends with the grail to heaven.

The saintly Galahad's ascension contrasts with his worldly father's encounter with the grail. In another tale, Sir Lancelot also visits the grail, but a voice warns him to withdraw from its presence. Ignoring the warning, Lancelot proceeds and is struck down like a dead man for twenty-four days, one day for every year he squandered without repentance. The moral of the story is straightforward—Christian virtue, not worldly honor, is the pathway to eternal glory.

Lancelot and Galahad both desire the grail, but only Galahad is worthy of it. Both overcome many obstacles to behold it, one guided by worldly standards and one by piety. This is an important point, because Lancelot is also a Christian knight who adheres to a code of honor. The problem is that he follows the lesser earthly good, sinking into many sins of the divided soul. He is in most ways an ideal knight, but his worldliness precludes him from achieving the greatest quest of all. Galahad, on the other hand, has a unified soul. He strives to be worthy of the prize he wants, which is communion with Christ. Galahad completes the quest because his desires are as pure and noble as his duties.

In the end Galahad succeeds because his desire for heaven motivates his duties on earth, demonstrating that hope upholds and uplifts effort. And this is where quest narratives overlap with the quotidian experiences of our ordinary lives. None of us is the chosen one—there are no Galahads among us. But we are all on a journey toward union with Christ. Most of us will live more like Hobbits than heroes, but we will certainly encounter dangers and temptations. I think this is why the Bible refers to the Christian life as a pilgrimage. Quests require struggle and sacrifice, and so do our everyday lives. But we do not labor in vain. When Galahad finds the grail, he gains what his heart desires, and we learn from him that endurance will eventually elevate our souls to God. However, quest narratives are not the only literary genre to examine the role of duty in the fulfilling of desire.

When I need a duty boost, I turn to Jane Austen. Austen's novels fall into the category called comedies of manners, which explore the customs, conventions, fashions, and follies of a particular social sphere. They are grounded in a specific time and place (in Austen's case, eighteenth-century Regency England), but explore universal themes such as love and identity. Because they are comedies, they end in marriage, so the complications of love are characteristically prominent.

But what do Austen's comedies of manners have in common with the Arthurian legend? Comedies of manners and heroic quests are linked by a common thread—in both genres, characters submerge desire within duty. In comedies of manners, duty is generally defined by obedience to social and moral conventions; in quest narratives, it is more often found in courageous and sacrificial action. In both cases, the duty is grueling and the desire is delayed, but in the end virtue is rewarded.

Published in 1811, Jane Austen's first novel, *Sense and Sensibility*, follows the genteel sisters, Elinor and Marianne Dashwood, who, along with their mother and little sister, have been left impoverished by the death of their father. Their spiteful and avaricious sister-in-law, Fanny, convinces her husband to break his promise to provide for his stepmother and sisters from the Dashwood estate. Instead, they cast them out of the family home to fend for themselves. They move into a tiny cottage on the property of Mrs. Dashwood's cousin, who welcomes them into their home and social circle. Because the Dashwood women have a strong and loving bond, they settle into their reduced lifestyle with a measure of contentment—until romantic complications befall them.

First, the dutiful Elinor grieves her separation from the young man she loves, Fanny's brother, Edward Ferrars. Their budding romance is interrupted not only by her father's death, but also by Fanny's cruel and vocal speculations that Elinor is after his money. She mourns her lost hopes in silence, channeling her energies into caring for her mother and sisters.

Meanwhile the desiring Marianne is falling madly in love with Mr. Willoughby, a handsome stranger who carries her home in his arms after she sprains her ankle on a solitary ramble. Marianne is dazzled by Willoughby, who shares her romantic tastes in poetry, art, and music. The two become inseparable, and Marianne flouts social propriety by exhibiting her affections without an official engagement announcement. With Willoughby around, she has no use for Colonel Brandon, the upright bachelor who also admires her. But disaster strikes—Willoughby suddenly disappears, called away by his wealthy aunt (as he says) on business. Unlike Elinor, the dejected Marianne does not suffer in silence, but gives way to her wounded feelings with a great deal of what we moderns might call adolescent drama.

The novel continues to highlight the differences between the sisters as they navigate disappointment. As the title suggests, Elinor embodies sense, and Marianne sensibility—used here as a synonym for emotion. But soon the problems increase. Elinor discovers that Edward is secretly engaged to the vulgar and vindictive Lucy Steele. Long ago he was attracted by Lucy's superficial charms, and now he is bound by his sense of honor to maintain their hasty engagement even though he no longer cares for her. To make matters worse, the artful Lucy, seeing Edward's preference for Elinor, confides her secret to Elinor and binds her to secrecy. Elinor's dutiful spirit determines her response. Her love for Edward increases with her respect for his character and compassion for his dilemma, but to keep her promise she must hold her sufferings inside. Romantic calamity also befalls Marianne when she learns that Willoughby is actually engaged to a rich heiress. In contrast to Elinor, Marianne falls into a state of complete collapse, relying on her sister for comfort and support. Elinor bears it in silence.

Like Galahad, Elinor always makes the right choice. She is prudent, gentle, courteous, and patient. Marianne is more like Lancelot; she embodies Austen's perceptions of the romantic follies of her age. Modern screen adaptations of *Sense and Sensibility* tend to portray the sisters as equally imbalanced—Marianne may be too histrionic, but Elinor is too repressed. But that is not Austen's perspective. In the pages of the novel Elinor is the undisputed heroine of the story. When all is revealed between them, Marianne is aghast. "Four months!" cried Marianne again. "So calm! So cheerful! How have you been supported?"

"By feeling I was doing my duty."[3]

This is insufficient for the desire-driven Marianne. She minimizes her sister's feelings, but Elinor vocalizes the depth of her pain.

> *"I understand you. You do not suppose that I have ever felt much... The composure of mind with which I have brought myself at present to consider the matter, the consolation that I have been willing to admit, have been the effect of constant and painful exertion;—they did not spring up*

---

3. Austen, *Sense and Sensibility*, 246.

of themselves;-- they did not occur to relieve my spirits at first.— No, Marianne.—THEN, if I had not been bound to silence, perhaps nothing could have kept me entirely—not even what I owed to my dearest friends—from openly shewing that I was VERY unhappy."[4]

At this Marianne repents of her selfish judgments.

"Oh! Elinor," she cried, "you have made me hate myself for ever.—How barbarous have I been to you!—you, who have been my only comfort, who have borne with me in all my misery, who have seemed to be only suffering for me!— Is this my gratitude?—Is this the only return I can make you?—Because your merit cries out upon myself, I have been trying to do it away."[5]

This is the moment of reconciliation. Just as Galahad's Christian virtue triumphs over Lancelot's worldly honor, so does Elinor's humane sense harmonize Marianne's erratic sensibilities. Like Galahad, Elinor has a unified soul, capable of both deep attachment and steadfast endurance.

More than 150 years after Austen's comedies of manners were written, Flannery O'Connor's book of essays, *Mystery and Manners*, argues that the most profound literary inflection point is the exploration of the mysteries of the human condition which are always hidden beneath conventional manners of individuals or societies. What the world sees are our manners, but who we really are is often a mystery,

---

4. Austen, *Sense and Sensibility*, 247.
5. Ibid.

even (or especially) to ourselves. O'Connor was fascinated by the gap between mystery and manners and so was Austen. Underneath Elinor's impeccable manners lies the most inscrutable mystery of all: the agonies of the innocent. Why do the righteous suffer? Why do the wicked prosper? What is this world in which Lucy Steele and Mr. Willoughby seem to prevail?

This mystery haunts literature because it haunts everything. A story that confronts the problem of evil from a Christian perspective is called a *theodicy*. The goal of a theodicy is "to justify the ways of God to men."[6] Flannery O'Connor's theodicies confront evil in what she called "large and startling figures."[7] Her fiction is populated by murderers, misfits, deviants, and degenerates. The Arthurian legend takes another approach, symbolizing the concept of evil in dragons, enchantments, and other monstrous presences. But Austen weaves evil into the ordinary, which is most often how we encounter it. Her comedies of manners are a kind of theodicy, portraying human folly and wickedness in their most common and therefore their most insidious guises—pettiness, spite, envy, gossip, competition, greed, unforgiveness, disdain, and other sins of everyday life that manifest the divisions of our souls. The drawing rooms of Regency England are Austen's battlefields, and the great-souled Elinor Dashwood is her Galahad.

Like Sir Galahad, Elinor receives her reward. In the end Lucy Steele runs away with another man, releasing Edward

---

6. Milton, *Paradise Lost*, 1.26.
7. O'Connor, "The Fiction Writer and His Country," in *Mystery and Manners: Occasional Prose*, 34.

from his obligation and freeing him to declare his love for Elinor. Then she marries a man as honorable as she is. Both are unified souls, and each is the other's reward.

But what of Marianne? The fickle Willoughby always regrets that he abandoned Marianne, but she does not suffer the same fate: the steadfast Colonel Brandon wins her heart. Brandon is the proper match for Marianne, whose desiring soul is not complete in itself. Colonel Brandon's steadfast sense harmonizes Marianne's tempestuous sensibilities, and her joyful spirit enlivens Brandon's staid placidity. They are all perfectly happy, and the novel concludes, as all comedies do, in harmony and communion.

Like the genres we have explored in earlier chapters, heroic quests and comedies of manners reflect the cosmic reality of the comic impulse. These stories are icons of the Christian understanding that, as singer-songwriter Andrew Peterson puts it, "the world was good, the world is fallen, the world will be redeemed."[8] The characters in these tales sin and suffer, but virtue receives a glorious reward.

Stories like this depend on the same divine justice that characterizes tragedy, but in these tales that justice is multifaceted. Tragic justice is implacable, devoid of mitigating mercy. It is all the more severe because in a tragedy we are fully acquainted not only with the vices, but with the virtues and vulnerabilities of our central characters. We know them, perhaps even love them. We grieve when the avenging furies pursue Orestes or when Laertes pierces Hamlet with his poisoned sword. The *telos* of tragic justice is to punish and eradicate evil.

---

8. Peterson, "All Things New," *Resurrection Letters, Volume II*, track 4.

Such straightforward justice is softened in the Arthurian legend. In the order and hierarchy of the medieval imagination, justice must triumph in a quest as it does in a tragedy, but justice acts as a teacher as much as an executioner. Virtues are rewarded and vices are punished so that the knights will ultimately be aligned with the good.

Because of this, comic justice holds more space for human frailty. In *Sense and Sensibility*, Willoughby's carelessness and cupidity grievously wounds Marianne. Most readers are disgusted by his frat boy persona, but Willoughby is a fool, not a villain. By the end of the story he regrets his weakness, but he still attains a measure of happiness. "He lived to exert, and frequently to enjoy himself."[9] Even the manipulative Lucy Steele gets off pretty easily. She marries a wealthy husband and, although plagued by a lifetime of petty dramas, obtains the luxurious lifestyle she schemed so nastily to achieve.

Comic justice allows for these disparities, because the telos of a comedy is union, not division. Ultimately it matters far more that Elinor is rewarded than that Lucy Steele is punished. Justice shares space with mercy in a comic world.

These stories are icons of meaning in a frantic and demanding season. They remind me that the mundane duties of my quotidian life are transfigured by my desire for union with Christ. Ultimately the same virtues that ennoble Galahad to slay dragons enable me to load the dishwasher, and if we endure to the end, we receive the same eternal reward.

---

9. Austen, *Sense and Sensibility*, 353.

8

AGENTS AND OBJECTS

Feminine Desire in Literature

I was nine years old the first time a boy noticed me. I had transferred to a new school right before Christmas and in an attempt to learn my classmates' names, I volunteered to pass out homework folders. The boy's name was Brandon, and I still remember the way his eyes lit up when I slid his folder timidly across his desk. Later he asked if I would quiz him on the states and capitals, and we were the only students in the class to score 100% on the test. A few weeks later he left a box of chocolate-covered cherries and a real peacock feather on my desk. Readers, even at nine years old, I was a goner. By the time he held my hand at the skating rink on the last day of school, I was the happiest fourth grader in the state of California.

But the wheel of fortune turns, and it was not long before that man-eating succubus Jenny Watson came on the scene. She had blonde hair, french-rolled jeans, and a pair of white L.A. Gear high tops. I could not compete with Jenny Watson, and my ten-year-old heart was broken.

The thing I remember most is how differently I felt about

myself as a person in the world after recognizing that look in Brandon's eyes. Brandon was a child; the look was not "the male gaze" we hear so much about. It was more like a happy awareness of something marvelous. It came over me in an instant that this boy looked at me and considered me lovely. That startled me. In a wholly chaste way I discovered myself to be a person with the capacity to awaken desire. Of course I was not consciously aware of any of this, but nevertheless it marked a transformation in my self-conception. I began to reckon with the pleasures and pains of my feminine self in relation to the world.

In the Proverbs, King Solomon wrote that "the way of a man with a maid"[1] is a wondrous mystery. Plumbing that mystery is surely one reason why stories are so preoccupied with love. In Chapter 7 I examined the nature of comedy in light of the mystery of marriage. In this chapter I will address how gender, particularly femininity, is portrayed in stories, with a specific emphasis on the complexities of feminine and masculine desire in relation to one another.

At some point all men and women come to know themselves as gendered beings, and that realization is always accompanied by desire. At the proper time these desires include the desire for physical union, but are not limited to it. Between men and women exist many desires that are neither sexual nor sinful, but merely human, such as desires to be nurtured, admired, and loved. We want communion with the Other—to find ourselves desirable as a companion in his or her eyes.

---

1. Proverbs 30:19 (KJV).

For better or worse, desire is at the root of our identities as male or female. But desire without the safeguards of duty will tyrannize our passions. Throughout human history, stories explore the manifold ways duty and desire flow between men and women. But until the last 200 years or so, stories were for the most part invented or recorded by men. This means that the portrayal of fictional women for much of history has been largely filtered through the male mind—particularly through the potent force of masculine desire—impacting how we understand and experience feminine desire in the world.

One of the most intriguing stories about masculine desire is an ancient myth about a sculptor named Pygmalion who carves his ideal woman out of marble and falls in love with his own creation. The goddess, Venus, delighted by the unusual love story, rewards Pygmalion by transforming the statue into a living woman. Consequently Pygmalion and his enfleshed ideal live happily ever after. The myth conveys an enigma at the core of our topic—the masculine desire to invent a feminine ideal.

In 1912, British playwright George Bernard Shaw published his own version of Pygmalion in a play of the same name. Shaw's version features a phonetician Henry Higgins and his protege, Eliza Doolittle. Higgins wants to prove he is capable of transforming the graceless Cockney into a poised, eloquent woman by teaching her proper English. He succeeds, by Eliza's efforts as much as his own, but Higgins sees only his own accomplishment.

Shaw's play is based on the myth but is complicated by an ambivalent relationship between the central couple.

Higgins and Eliza do not marry, but they do form a bond. If not romantic, what is the nature of that bond? Higgins despises marriage but cares for Eliza. So what is it that he wants from her?

In fact, Eliza actually expects Higgins to woo her. When she asks him, "What did you do it for if you didn't care for me?" he answers: "Why, because it was my job."[2] He is not dodging the question; his response is the simple truth—Eliza Doolittle is the most impressive trophy of his distinguished career. When she threatens him with another suitor for her hand, Higgins jeers, "Can he make anything of you? That's the point."[3] To Pygmalion and Higgins, love, whether romantic or platonic, is inherently *creative*. The lover is the maker, and the beloved is the artifact.

Higgins is attached to Eliza not for her own sake but because she represents himself. His desire is not to promote her emerging selfhood, but through her to embody his own. This disordered dynamic often extends beyond the men in books to the men writing books. Fictional women almost always bear the weight of masculine desire in literature for the very valid reason that they do so in life. Their inadequate portrayal (when it happens) far too often reflects the divisions in the souls and societies of their authors. Eliza and characters like her expand beyond their literary context into a wider atmosphere of pervasive uncertainty about the desire of women. Eliza is not alone. The Western canon as a whole reflects a dizzying range of reactions to feminine desire. We are comfortable with women as *objects* but not

---

2. Shaw, *Pygmalion*, 101.
3. Shaw, *Pygmalion*, 102.

always as agents of desire.

One of the most authentic examinations of this dynamic is Sigrid Undset's 1928 Nobel prizewinning trilogy, *Kristin Lavransdatter*, which follows the tumultuous life of the eponymous heroine in medieval Norway. The eldest daughter of a respected nobleman, Lavrans Bjorgulfson, Kristin comes of age under the sheltering love of her honorable father, with whom she shares a special bond. Kristin is his favorite child, and on her he showers all the affectionate care of his noble heart. At the appropriate time he betroths her to a neighboring landowner, Simon Darre, whose temperament and character are much like his own. Lavrans knows that with Simon, Kristin will continue the pious and protected life of her childhood. The docile Kristin is content with the arrangement until she goes to live at a convent in Oslo where she meets the ardent Erlend Nikulaussøn and everything changes. They begin a passionate romance that sets the course of Kristin's life. Erlend seduces Kristin. Soon he coerces her to meet for assignations at a brothel, convinces her to terminate her engagement to Simon, and even involves her in the death of his former mistress. Rumors of this reach Lavrans, but he refuses to believe them. He cannot reconcile these whispered hints of a reckless, passionate young woman with his image of Kristin as a pure and pious maiden. His wife, Ragnfrid, is more discerning. After Kristin returns home from the convent, Ragnfried perceives that Kristin has changed and suggests that at least some of the rumors might be true. She advises Lavrans to consider allowing them to marry based on the possibility that Kristin has yielded her virginity, but Lavrans lashes out at her.

> *Have you taken leave of your senses? How can you think such things of our good, beautiful child? Nothing much can have happened to her there, with the nuns. I know she's no milkmaid who gives up her virtue behind a fence. You must realize that she can't have seen this man or spoken to him more than a few times. She'll get over him...Here at home on my own farm I can surely protect my own daughter. And I don't believe any maiden of good family and with an honorable and Christian upbringing would part so easily with her honor or her life.*[4]

Immediately after his angry outburst, Lavrans begins to press Ragnfrid about a past lover, lamenting that he has not understood his wife since early in their marriage when she desired more sexual connection that he felt he was able to give.

> *"When you wanted me to be toward you—in a way that I couldn't . . . Were you thinking about the other man then?" he whispered, frightened and confused and tormented.*[5]

The abrupt shift between his denial about his daughter and his anxiety over his wife has a melancholy logic to it. His worry over Kristin stirs up the sorrows of his marriage. Lavrans is a dutiful man who has never reckoned with the reality that wife and daughter are sensual women. He protects and provides for them on the terms he understands, which are insufficient to the complexities of their divided

---

4. Undset, *Kristin Lavransdatter: The Wreath*, 206-207.
5. Undset, *Kristin Lavransdatter: The Wreath*, 207.

souls. Of course, Lavrans, too, is a divided soul. He is honorable and sincere, but willfully blind to the actuality of sexual brokenness in his family. His insistence on limiting the scope of his vision leaves Ragnfrid and Kristin to grapple with their desires without him. They do this in different ways, Kristin by falling into the arms of a man in every way opposite to her father, and Ragnfried by quietly withdrawing herself from intimacy while acting the part of a dutiful wife. Lavrans is left in the no man's land between.

Erlend, on the other hand, ignites Kristin's desires so he can fulfill his own. Although he plans to marry her in the future, he is unwilling to honor his duty before slaking his appetites, which creates confusion in Kristin and chaos in their community. After Kristin rejects Simon, she begs Lavrans to allow her to marry Erlend, but when her father learns of Erlend's checkered past, he refuses outright. He considers Erlend unreliable and unworthy, and he assures Kristin that she will forget him in time. But she and Erlend have gone too far for simplistic separation tactics. By this time Erlend's claim on Kristin is absolute. Her heart is the battleground between her father's duty and her lover's desires.

Meanwhile, Kristin is far more than a prize to be won. Her inner life is as vivid and complex as her headstrong actions. Because of her beauty and her gentleness, Lavrans and Erlend are often bewildered by what seems to them to be incomprehensible defiances and demands. Shortly after they are married, Erlend is surprised by Kristin's self-will.

Never would I have believed, Kristin—during all the time I was courting you, rushing around and begging my kinsmen to speak on my behalf and making myself so meek and pitiful in order to win you—that you could be such a witch![6]

Kristin is not an ideal woman; she is a real one. She is deeply flawed and deeply good. Over the course of their complicated marriage, Erlend discovers what Lavrans did—that Kristin's divided soul takes up as much room in their lives as his. Both Erlend and Lavrans love her, but they struggle to accept that she is not only the object of their opposing desires, but an agent of her own. Like Pygmalion, they cast her into their ideal woman, but she will never be an animated projection of her father or her husband's expectations.

I think feminine desire baffles everyone. I am often as confused by my own desiring soul as anybody. What do I want? I want to eat ice cream and I want to be thin. I want to work and I want to rest. I want to make love and I want to be left alone. I want help and I want independence. I want attention and I want solitude. I want to be desirable and I want to be chaste. I want to be strong and I want to be rescued. I am a mystery to myself and to others. More than the men I know, I seem to always want contradictory things. A book about my divided soul would be as vast and varied as *Kristin Lavransdatter*.

So what are we to do with feminine desire? Nobody really knows, and neither do the books. Lavrans and Erlend represent common opposing masculine responses to feminine desire—the first of which is to restrict it, the second to

---

6. Undset, *Kristin Lavransdatter: The Wife*, 316.

exploit it. Both cause damage, and neither succeeds. Kristin's personhood transcends both disordered attempts to overpower her desiring soul.

But is it too simplistic to condemn masculine desire as naive or controlling? I think there is something universal underlying the Pygmalion urge. Let us turn once again to the very first story. God created Adam in his own image. Adam is himself an artifact of love, commanded to imitate his creator. And because "it is not good for the man to be alone"[7] the very first creative act Adam participates in is the making of a woman, who was "taken out of man."[8] God fashioned Eve from Adam's rib, leaving a gap in the masculine self. The divine wound beneath Adam's heart was Eve's ground-of-being.

On a symbolic level, this is astonishing. Women exist because of a cosmic division of man from himself, and this does not cut both ways. Yes, a woman suffers to give birth to sons and daughters, but that comes later and its ramifications are different. In forming Eve, God Himself inflicts the wound in Adam's flesh even *before* the fall. When Eve is created, she is complete in herself—but Adam is not. His only hope of wholeness is to unite himself with the woman created from him. Therefore Adam is vulnerable because he cannot help but desire her, but if Eve does not desire him in return, he remains incomplete. And because all of this happened before the fall, it means that this is the way men and women were made to be.

The difference between Adam and Pygmalion is funda-

---

7. Genesis 2:18 (KJV).
8. Genesis 2:23 (KJV).

mental. For Pygmalion, love is creative; for Christians, Love is the Creator. The sculptor's beloved is only an image of himself enfleshed in marble and enlivened by the goddess of desire. In falling in love with his statue, he worships his own desires, more like masturbation than marriage. But Adam's love story is entirely different. Eve was indeed taken out of Adam, but he did not make her. God made her. From the beginning Eve was a separate self, an Other who was also a Counterpart—a "helper suitable for him."[9] Adam and Eve were given to one another, whole and holy, by God. Only this beginning can ever be a secure foundation for abiding intimacy and ennobling love.

The masculine urge to love a woman created from himself is a legacy from Eden. It is not wicked in itself, but it *is* corrupted by the fall. On earth we will never know what that dynamic was intended to be, but we do know its dark side. The fallen masculine soul will always be tempted to deny or dominate feminine desire and to relegate women to objects because the masculine soul is rendered vulnerable by women as agents. Out of the divided souls of men come many disordered projections of false feminine ideals, from fainting Victorian ingenues to insatiable pop culture bombshells. The fallen man will always objectify the virgin and the vamp.

But that is only the fallen part of men. Underneath all the false images lies a right longing to awaken and satisfy a real woman. When Adam meets Eve, he rejoices because she is "bone of my bone and flesh of my flesh."[10] The next

---

9. Genesis 2:18 (KJV).
10. Genesis 2:23 (KJV).

words speak to the immense power of a woman in the life of a man.

> *Therefore shall a man leave his father and mother,*
> *And shall cleave unto his wife,*
> *And they shall be one flesh.*[11]

To unite himself with a real woman, a man will leave all former things behind. The urge to project himself upon her will give way to the aspiration to share himself with her, to know her and to be known by her. It is a great triumph of the devil that so many deny or exploit feminine desire, because the desire of women can restore worlds. All of us instinctively recognize this in literature and life. The mysterious undulations of desire in Eve, Eliza Doolittle, Kristin Lavransdatter, and countless others determine the fate of the men in the stories. It seems to me that our ambivalence toward feminine desire exists because it is at once the most potent and the most fragile human instinct in the world.

To complicate matters even more, feminine desire was cursed at the fall, a curse Eve brought upon herself by severing the link between duty and desire when she broke the commandment. The self-made curse is that "your desire shall be for your husband and he shall rule over you"[12] Adam's most fundamental human need, his wife's desire for him, becomes the most fractured aspect of her humanity. Thus women, too, are wounded by their own disordered desires for men. Her desire was intended to heal him, but

---

11. Genesis 2:24 (KJV).
12. Genesis 3:16 (KJV).

instead it damages them both. Every story ever told about men and women wrestles with the universal grief of this broken communion, portraying flawed men and women struggling to find their way as damaged people in a damaged world. We need these stories, because they offer insight into important realities.

This means that we cannot shy away from literary portrayals of foolish and wicked women (even when written by men) because they tell the truth about the fallen world. There is a great difference between a robust character who is realistically flawed and a flat character who conveys a false image of femininity. Neither are all idealized feminine archetypes false images. Many are not related to disordered desire at all but are analogues to eternal realities.

Consider, for example, a princess in a fairy tale. Princesses represent both the soul and the cosmos, which are always feminine in Christian tradition. In keeping with the divided soul of our age, too many modern retellings of fairy tales emasculate or excise the role of the prince, which violates the archetypal narrative and ultimately fails to produce a believable or satisfying story. We may read some rave reviews from revisionist critics, but after the buzz dwindles, the mangled tale thankfully fizzles into obscurity. Why? Attempts to deconstruct fairy tales flop because the whole point of a fairy tale is that a princess, like the soul and the world, cannot save herself, but must be rescued by intervening love.

In 1964 Shaw's *Pygmalion* was adapted into the smash hit musical comedy film, *My Fair Lady*. The characters and conflicts remain the same, but the ending is completely different. In Shaw's play Eliza asserts her independence from Henry and leaves him—but audiences and performers never liked the ending, and so *My Fair Lady* ends with the couple falling in love instead. Unlike *Pygmalion*, the film mimics the narrative pattern of the Beauty and the Beast fairy tale, in which the princess (Eliza) tames the monster (Henry) with her love, revealing his true form after he transplants the princess from persecution and deprivation to safety and abundance. Eliza makes him good; Henry makes her happy. Shaw's attempt to subvert the fairy tale archetype miscarries because he misjudged the power of the narrative. We *want* Henry and Eliza to fall in love. We instinctively recognize that the prince and the princess belong together, that Henry and Eliza are missing an essential quality of happiness if he does not win her heart. Ultimately the film tells a truer story than the play, because we all long to see the union between men and women restored.

Marriage brings men and women together in the sacramental union of duty and desire, but desire is inevitably complicated. Duty purifies and orients desire. True duty cannot be corrupted; it can only be misunderstood and misapplied. This is important because authentic duty may sting in the moment, but it never inflicts lasting damage. Distortions of duty are rampant though. Lavrans is honorable, but he fails to discern and enact his proper duty to his daughter. He should have faced the truth about Kristin and Erlend and acted accordingly. Henry's selfish desire to create a woman in his own image precludes his ability to love her for herself, corrupting their relationship and wounding them both. Between men and women in our time lies a wasteland of distorted desire, and to bring it back to life we need to return to our true duties to one another. There is much at stake in the desire-saturated spirit of our age.

The virtue that harmonizes duty and desire between the genders is chastity, which means far more than sexual abstinence. Chastity is earthy and robust. It aligns our erotic desires to their proper objects and restrains them from their potential for destruction. But chastity is not abstract—it is not an ethereal concept or idea that happens only within the mind. Chastity is itself sensual and embodied. It is put to work in the world as either celibacy or marriage. Celibacy is the erotic state of the unmarried, a state characterized by restraint and honor, when sensual urges are transfigured into other forms of reciprocal care. All relationships between men and women are celibate, with only one proper exception. Marriage is the erotic state of sexual union between one man and one woman, both fulfilling and limiting the duty and desire of each spouse. In addition, chastity makes possible an appropriate level of intimacy between men and women in other relationships. When men and women are chaste, they can enjoy flourishing and dignifying relationships with one another. When they are not, disorder and destruction ensues.

Chastity also governs the duties and desires of procreation. Like the banks of a river, it rims and directs our tumultuous desires, transforming wild torrents into fruitful waters. Because of its boundaries, we bear and rear children who are beloved and secure. Violations of chastity have consequences on succeeding generations, inflicting wounds in need of remedy. For the most part, it is desire that propels procreation and duty that enacts it. This brings us back to the enigmas of desire between men and women. God carved a holy wound in Adam to open him to the delights and dependencies of love, and he created Eve from beneath Adam's heart, whole in herself, to turn toward him of her own will. Desire draws them together. Neither masculine nor feminine desires are sufficient in themselves; they unite with one another in the bonds of sacred duties to bring forth new life.

This is the way things are supposed to be, but more often than not our lives fall short, and that is why books like *Kristin Lavransdatter* are so important. Like all real-life marriages, Kristin and Erlend's relationship fractures along the faultlines of their divided souls. From the outside looking in, they seem to have transcended their early missteps—they are attractive, amorous, rich, prestigious, powerful, and fecund with their eight sons—but underneath the veneer are two fragile souls whose passions taint their bond. Erlend continues to be immoderate and indulgent, and Kristin despises him for the very attributes that once cajoled her into bed. She cannot muster the trust and respect properly forged by shared principles, but the center of their marriage holds because their mutual desire, although corruptible, remains an essential adhesive. As Kristin's erotic tumult attests, it is no wonder that feminine desire is as murky and perplexing in literature as it is in life, and stories like *Kristin Lavransdatter* convey the power and complexity of feminine desire.

All of this has implications for more general creativity. There is, so to speak, a chastity of the creative as well the procreative impulse. When a writer creates a character, that imaginary being is entirely subject to its creator. Writers abuse this power all the time, crafting bad characters in bad stories for bad reasons. Most of the time these stories are culled from the literary record in a natural way, but many disordered projections of feminine desire remain. Widespread pressure notwithstanding, we cannot expunge these from the literary record, nor should we try. But we can choose something better. When a male writer plays Pygmalion with his female characters, he does violence to himself, to women, and to art. Man may be made in the image of God, but no man is actually God, which means authors write better stories when they resist the temptation to idealize, villainize, or reduce the divided souls of their female characters.

But female authors are not exempt. Too many contemporary writers complain about problematic female characters but fail to recognize that their demands for women to be portrayed in a certain way ("strong," "complex," "powerful") to the exclusion of any other way is just another bullying attempt to subjugate women (in this case fictional ones) into submission to external standards. Such efforts demean women and degrade storytelling. But creative chastity submits to the intrinsic goodness of gendered beings by portraying them honestly and charitably in accordance with the terms of reality.

Ultimately, just as I did when I was nine, I do want to behold that look of astounded delight from masculine eyes. I think probably all men and women want that from one another. Only chastity makes it possible, even sacred. What would it take to recall us to that sense of wondrous self-giving in the presence of the Other? I often wonder if we tell stories about desire in an attempt to recover and reach for those luminous moments. Both feminine and masculine desire are ultimately eschatological—they exist to draw us to one another and beyond one another toward the righteous communion we will share in the kingdom of God. In the end, all chaste longing between men and women will be fulfilled, and longing itself will converge toward God, the Lover of our Souls, Who Is both the Agent and the Object of all desire.

9

FORMAL LONGING

Duty and Desire in Poetry

When I was a sophomore in college, I discovered the poetry of Rainer Maria Rilke. I would sit on the dock of the university's arboretum lake, my legs dangling over the silver water as the frogs sang. Above my head stretched the knotted limbs of midwest oak and elm, ancient trees heavy with fresh leaves amidst the wet Indiana spring. Under those trees, I read Rilke's poems.

> *Again and again, however we know the landscape of love*
> *and the little churchyard there, with its sorrowing names,*
> *and the frighteningly silent abyss into which the others*
> *fall: again and again the two of us walk out together*
> *under the ancient trees, lie down again and again*
> *among the flowers, face to face with the sky.*[1]

At that time, I was already learning the grief and glory of what it means to love, but I had no interior language through

---

1. Rainer Maria Rilke, "Again and again, however we know the landscape of love," trans. Stephen Mitchell.

which to interpret the baffling complexity of it. The poems solved nothing, yet by that midwestern lake, an image took root in my mind that lurks there still: lovers gazing at the sky under the arching limbs of old trees whose implacable roots absorb them into the fertile ground. This image of twinned love and death haunted me then as it does now, but I had no grasp of what I was reading. It was an image, nothing more. I did not yet know that at the intersection of my adolescent angst and Rilke's poem, I was encountering a great mystery, found in another poem, far more ancient.

> *Set me as a seal upon your heart,*
> *as a seal upon your arm,*
> *for love is strong as death,*
> *jealousy is fierce as the grave.*
> *Its flashes are flashes of fire,*
> *the very flame of the Lord.*
> *Many waters cannot quench love,*
> *Neither can floods drown it.*
> *If a man offered for love*
> *all the wealth of his house,*
> *He would be utterly despised.*[2]

Now I know that *love is as strong as death*, but then I knew only an image of lovers under trees. To my sophomore mind, the image was isolated, even personal, but now I know that it was actually a signpost of the transcendence embedded within the ambiguity of the poem. Indeed, the ambiguity

---

2. Song of Songs 8:6-7 (ESV).

was the language of the mystery itself.

In previous chapters we have looked at how stories contemplate our divided souls; in this chapter I will examine how poetry does it. A story can be mysterious, but a narrative does not trade in ambiguity as poetry does. People tell me all the time that they don't really "get" poetry, and that's fair, but the mystery of a poem is purposeful because poems delve into the granular particularity of human experience, which is a mystery to us all—and the most fundamental mystery on earth is our divided souls.

Poetry has so often been called "the language of desire" that I have no idea who said it first. I think perhaps poetry succeeds at capturing the agony and ecstasy of a myriad of human desires better than any other creative form, except possibly song—which is, after all, poetry in harmony. But why? What is it about poetry that lends itself to longing?

When I try to answer this question definitively, I find my mind tied up in knots, and then I begin to wonder if the tangling and untangling of knots is itself a profound image for poetry. If the elements of poetry are strands of contemplation, a poem becomes a tapestry that embodies a condensed image of the divided soul. Like a weaver, the poet stands at the loom, shuttle at work, weaving the strands of reality and imagination, structure and meaning, duty and desire into an artistic tapestry.

Like poetry, weaving is governed by rules. One of the oldest crafts in human history, every culture in the history of the world has a rich weaving tradition—as Scott and I discovered while on a Mediterranean cruise for our ten year anniversary. In Turkey, we were required, like all tourists, to attend a rug demonstration. I did not know what to expect, but I was entranced. Picture a line of women at huge wooden looms, their hair tied back, their brows knit in concentration, their fingers flying across the long, white, flexible strands, tying tiny knots of wool or silk, row by row, column by column. We learned that weaving a single rug can take years, sometimes even a decade, because of the meticulous nature of the work.

Writing a poem is like this. Every poet must reckon with the vast poetic tradition, assimilating extensive knowledge and skill into his personal efforts. Just as a weaver cannot make a beautiful tapestry without learning to tie tiny strings and knots in prescribed patterns of color, line, and shape, so a poet must learn to select suitable formal elements of syntax, structure, and style. The poet may take up his art to express his own interior experiences, but he cannot do so with any meaningful skill until he submits to the craft of poetry. In other words, the art of poetry functions as the duty that harmonizes the divided soul of a poem, while desire is the mystery that makes the poem meaningful.

To illustrate, let us examine a moment in one of the greatest poems in the world: The *Iliad*. The first time we encounter Helen of Troy, she is weaving.

> *Now to Helen of the white arms, came a messenger, Iris . . .*
> *She came on Helen in the chamber; she was weaving a great web,*
> *A red folding robe, and weaving into it the numerous struggles*
> *Of Trojans, breakers of horses, and strong-armed Achaians,*
> *Struggles that they endured for her sake at the hands of the war gods.*[3]

---

3. Homer, The *Iliad*, 3.121,125–128.

Formal Longing

    In this scene, Iris, the messenger goddess, has come to deliver a message to Helen, who stands at a loom, weaving stories from the war into a robe. As the war rages outside her chamber window, she contemplates the chaos and destruction by creating something from it. She makes a meaningful artifact that unites her particular experience with a universal phenomenon. Since time immemorial, humans have been crafting artifacts to reflect their inner contemplations of the outer world. We call it art.

    But what is her art about? You will remember that Helen is the most beautiful of women, the daughter of Zeus, and the wife of Menalaus, King of Sparta. But Helen has suffered a crisis of desire. Nearly ten years before Iris's visit, Helen meets Paris, Prince of Troy, who has come to their homeland of Sparta on a diplomatic mission. At the time Helen does not know that the goddess Aphrodite is plotting to fulfill her promise to give Paris the most beautiful woman in the world as his wife. The goddess sends her son, Eros, to shoot Paris and Helen with his devastating arrows. Immediately they fall madly in love and Paris lures Helen away from her lawful husband to dwell with him in Troy. In response, Menelaus and his brother, King Agamemnon, muster the Greeks and launch a fleet of a thousand ships to besiege Troy and restore unfaithful Helen to her husband.

    It is now nine years into the war, and Helen is still all but chained to Paris' bed. She still finds Paris irresistible but is constantly tormented by what she has done and what she has lost. Desire has devastated her life, her family, and her entire land. There is no action she can take to free herself. She begs to return to her former life, but in response

Aphrodite fetches Paris from the battlefield to her bedchamber and threatens to kill her if she does not welcome him to bed. She consents. Helen is trapped in a wasteland of conflicting desires.

She turns to her loom. As she weaves, she weeps and talks about her sadness to anybody who will listen: her serving women, King Priam, Prince Hector, her lover, Paris. The robe she weaves depicts the men she sees from the windows of her chamber dying in battle for her sake.

This is profound enough, but there's more. Zooming out, we see that Helen's robe is part of a larger artifact, the *Iliad*, which is itself about soldiers who died for Helen's sake. Like Helen, Homer created a formal artifact—an epic poem—which serves the same purpose as the woven robe: to meditate upon the mysteries of the divided soul. The tapestry and the epic are each woven skillfully out of strands of reality and imagination, structure and meaning, duty and desire. Here again, poetry is the language of desire expressed through the grammar of formal duty.

Like Helen's tapestry, poetry is constructed of technical elements woven together to form an artifact. This is the dutiful part of a poem. Throughout this book we have looked at how our moral, relational, and spiritual duties harmonize the energy of our desires. So it is with poetry. Without the structural limits enforced by the technical aspects of poetry, the transcendent longing it illuminates remains an inarticulate jumble of disconnected experiences, images, and ideas. Form is the scaffolding for meaning. Poetry portrays desire, but the desiring soul of a poem cannot exist unless it adheres to the duties of structure, syntax, and style, just as the image on a tapestry cannot exist without the methodical tying of strings and knots. Structure and meaning cohere into a whole.

This is also true from another angle. The formal scaffolding of poetry, although essential, cannot stand alone. The purpose of a scaffold is to uphold something great or useful or beautiful, and in a poem, that something is a constellation of meaning-making ideas, experiences, images, or contemplations connected somehow with the longings of the human heart. There are plenty of poems that are technically proficient but artistically underwhelming, failing to reach beyond the formal into the mysterious. Ultimately the structure exists to support the meaning, not vice versa.

This is a profoundly important idea because as moral beings, we crave a moral center. Some of us conform to it, some of us resist it—all of us rely on it. But the Christian moral vision is defined by desire far more than duty. Christ tells the disciples that He came not that they may have many rules, which they already had under the Old Covenant, but "that they may have life and have it abundantly."[4] We do not keep the commandments to earn gold stars on a cosmic checklist, but by keeping the commandments we participate in the life of Christ on earth in the hope of attaining the Kingdom of God. The life of Christ is the blessed life, because Christ is our life now and forever.

This is the way of poetry, and I think it is what the mystic St. Porphyrios was getting at when he said, "Whoever wants to become a Christian must first become a poet."[5]

---

4. John 10:10 (ESV).
5. Saint Porphyrios, *Wounded by Love: The Life and Wisdom of Saint Porphyrios*, 107.

The commandments, or duties, of poetry are myriad, but they exist as scaffolding for desire. Another way of saying this is that the *telos* of a poem is not technical expertise, although technique provides the necessary framework for the desiring heart of a poem. But when a poem is harmonized between the duties of form and the desires of the heart, it "hales souls out of men's bodies."[6]

This is true for every poem, including secular ones, because like all created things, poetry reflects its makers, which in turn reflects their Maker. And this brings us back to the question of poetry's ambiguity, which holds back so many readers from its riches. Everybody knows that poetry is obscure. It does not reveal its secrets without struggle. In fact, to the utter incredulity of the concrete mind, poetry is mysterious *on purpose*. But what purpose does that serve? Why read and write poetry at all?

If the answer to that question is that poetry should posit propositional truths and moral maxims that fix the problems of our divided souls, poets should hang up their hats. But propositional truth and moral maxims are not the point of poetry. The point of poetry is to contemplate mystery. Notice the word *contemplate*, rather than *explain* or *understand*. Contemplation assumes a humble and meditative posture. To accomplish this purpose, poems pose universal questions about our divided souls by concentrating on particular experiences. Thus, poetry's ambiguity is its strength, because its elusive nature allows it to be the medium of a myriad of meditations on life's mysteries.

---

6. Shakespeare, *Much Ado About Nothing*, 2.3.60.

Consider how the following two poems contemplate desire in contrasting ways.

The Crazed Moon
W.B. Yeats

Crazed through much child-bearing
The moon is staggering in the sky;
Moon-struck by the despairing
Glances of her wandering eye
We grope, and grope in vain,
For children born of her pain.
Children dazed or dead!
When she in all her virginal pride
First trod on the mountain's head
What stir ran through the countryside
Where every foot obeyed her glance!
What manhood led the dance!
Fly-catchers of the moon,
Our hands are blenched, our fingers seem
But slender needles of bone;
Blenched by that malicious dream
They are spread wide that each
May rend what comes in reach.[7]

---

7. W. B. Yeats, "The Crazed Moon."

Astrophil and Stella 31: With how sad steps, O Moon, thou climb'st the skies
Sir Philip Sidney

With how sad steps, O Moon, thou climb'st the skies!
How silently, and with how wan a face!
What, may it be that even in heav'nly place
That busy archer his sharp arrows tries!
Sure, if that long-with love-acquainted eyes
Can judge of love, thou feel'st a lover's case,
I read it in thy looks; thy languish'd grace
To me, that feel the like, thy state descries.
Then, ev'n of fellowship, O Moon, tell me,
Is constant love deem'd there but want of wit?
Are beauties there as proud as here they be?
Do they above love to be lov'd, and yet
Those lovers scorn whom that love doth possess?
Do they call virtue there ungratefulness?[8]

As you can see, the moon is the subject of each poem's meditation on desire, but Yeats and Sidney portray her in unique ways. In Yeats' poem, the murderous moon makes humanity complicit in destructive action. Sidney, on the other hand, renders the moon as a beacon of grief in the face of wayward human will. The moon is the same; the meaning is altogether different, even directly opposed. If the poems were tapestries, the first tapestry would depict men in hellish contortions under the moon as a leering orb, and the other as inconstant lovers overseen by a mournful,

---

8. Sidney, *Astrophil and Stella*.

Formal Longing

but removed, celestial light. Both are the moon, but they are not the same vision of the moon.

Yet in spite of the divergent portrayals, everybody recognizes the moon. The moon is generic. She is a thread of material reality that anchors the poems to something tangible. Each poem weaves her in a particular manner that befits the underlying reflections of the poem. And although the two visions of the moon are frankly irreconcilable, we accept both. We recognize that both poems, in spite of their ambiguities, present perspectives that *work*. How can that be? Gazing into the contradictions of these two poems underscores the powerful, albeit mysterious, function of poetry: its capacity to contemplate the universal reality of the divided soul through particular experiences of it.

When I say that poetry contemplates universals through particulars, I mean that it meditates upon transcendent ideas, or *universals*, by comparing and contrasting them to earth-bound experiences, or *particulars*. Particulars are concrete, while universals are abstract. Thus, Rilke's lovers under the trees are concrete, while love and death are abstract. Sidney's moonlit musings are particular, while his meditations on human will and overseeing deity are universal. That is why we accept both versions of the moon. It is because the moon is not the point; the moon is only the vehicle, or the particular concrete image that beguiles us into the universal contemplation.

This leads us into the realm of analogy, which is poetry's ground of being. Through analogy, poetry asks the question, "How is a particular something, X, like a universal something else, Y?" Usually the X is an object or experience, like the moon or the keeping of bees or lovers entwined under trees. The Y, then, is a concept or idea, like death or beauty or falling in love.

Far from being simply a literary device, then, analogy is the grammar of transcendence. It is the way humans express words and images to reach beyond ourselves into the mysteries of the divided soul: love, suffering, hope, grief, desire. We encounter something very simple, like moonlight or old trees, that somehow accesses our universal longing for unity within ourselves and grief at our ongoing division. Poets transform those moments of wonder into poetry, the artifact of mystery. They are the images woven into the tapestry.

But the point of a poem is not the same as the point of a tapestry. A tapestry portrays a clear image, but a poem? Ah, a poem has a more elusive *telos*: a poem must point beyond itself into the mystery of the human condition. If the point is to contemplate mystery through particular experience, then a poem reaches from the dust of earth toward holy ground.

Eventually every analogy reaches its limit. It is, after all, merely strings and knots. Therefore, any poem worth its salt maintains its mystery on purpose, which means it must be, as we come full circle, ambiguous. Poetry's ambiguity is its glory, because ambiguity is the formal expression of mystery. The point of a poem is to gaze into the mystery of how the things of earth connect to whatever exists beyond it.

Christians call this incarnation. A poem incarnates life's mysteries through a sequence of carefully chosen words enfleshed in formal poetic elements. The bones and sinews are the form and structure of the poem, and the blood and skin are what is expressed through language and imagery. The result is a contemplation of universal mysteries through particular language and form. When Christ incarnated Himself, he did not just become man, but a *particular* man. He became Yeshua the Nazarene, born into a specific time and place in history. Jesus lived and died on planet Earth as a particular person as well as the universal Messiah. The Incarnation is Word-made-flesh, the union of earth and heaven, the consummation of what art yearns to imitate.

Incarnation is the seminal reason why St. Porphyrios believed that a Christian must be a poet. Significantly, the canon of poetry as a whole understands the incarnation of Christ as a preeminent mystery—the Deep Magic, as C.S. Lewis called it. The staggering number of poems that have been written about the impossible paradox of the Incarnation proves that enfleshing words is a transformative human experience. What's more, the more specific and personal the incarnation, the more transcendent and universal becomes the resulting contemplation. Consider, for instance, the meaning of the shape of the cross over time. No longer is it an ancient torture device in the common imagination. Incarnation made it a universal symbol of the Christian faith. When we incarnate a universal into a particular, it becomes both. That is the great risk and grace of poetry. I am not comparing Our Lord to a poem, but I am asserting that the One who Incarnated Himself wove into the human soul the capacity to imitate incarnation by embodying ideas in art, and in poetry we find a form that incarnates mystery with sublime precision.

The most mysterious and holy experience we can have with a poem is when it unlocks our latent longing for eternity. Rilke's poetry began its work on me on an Indiana college campus at age nineteen. Homer, Dante, Shakespeare, Donne, Blake, Herbert, Eliot, and Hopkins have all made me ache for something beyond this world that I cannot name but for which I would give everything. I cannot say how, but it happens when certain poems unlock an interior mystery, or what C.S. Lewis calls the "inconsolable secret."[9] It is poetry calling from earth into eternity, an invitation from our world into the world beyond.

This is such a poem for me.

Autumn
Rainer Maria Rilke

The leaves are falling, falling as if from far up,
as if orchards were dying high in space.
Each leaf falls as if it were motioning "no."
And tonight the heavy earth is falling
away from all other stars in the loneliness.

We're all falling. This hand here is falling.
And look at the other one. It's in them all.
And yet there is Someone, whose hands
infinitely gentle, hold up all this falling.[10]

---

9. Lewis, *The Weight of Glory and Other Addresses*, 29.
10. Rainer Maria Rilke, "Autumn."

Perhaps this poem means little to you, but I read it with blurred eyes and a lump in my throat every time, longing for the gentle hands of God to shelter me from plummeting into infinite loneliness. This is a great mystery of poetry—that one poem draws a soul to eternity while another does not. We cannot know which poems will stir the fragile veil between earth and heaven, but that is not the point. Not every poem is a window into the infinite for every soul. But we keep reading, because the point of a poem is to enlarge our contemplations of what it means to be human.

10

FORMS OF FIDELITY

Overcoming the Modern Tyranny of Desire

A handful of experiences from my childhood come to mind as I consider the foundations of my conception of duty and desire in society. The first is the 1988 presidential election. The air around me buzzed with bombastic claims that it was the most important election of our time, that a Republican victory would hold back the rising tide of moral decay. I was very young, and I believed every word. Lying awake at night, I prayed that the emissary of God, George H.W. Bush, would crush under his heel the malefactor, Michael Dukakis, and save us all from the moral relativism that was eroding the foundations of our nation. When I awoke on November 9 to the election results, I felt a conscious sense of security. The hero had overcome, and God still blessed America.

When the alarmist rhetoric returned in 1992, my political zeal was rekindled but this time the other side triumphed—and I felt the ground shift under my feet. I was a little bit older, but I still believed what I was told. The nation had betrayed the Founding Fathers, and God had given us over to our own wickedness. He would withdraw His blessing. I have never quite lost the bewilderment and insecurity of that moment.

Another formative memory took root during a third-grade school assembly when a martial arts expert taught us how to fend off kidnappers. Having gained crucial skills about how to spot a predator in a crowd and how to perform a motorcycle kick when grabbed from behind, I went forth in the knowledge that the streets of America are populated by pedophiles who lurk at every corner, biding their time until a child forgets to keep her head on a swivel.

I wish I could report that nobody ever actually tried to kidnap me. Later that same year while walking home from school, a heavyset man emerged from an idling station wagon parked at the narrow entrance of my cul-de-sac. I remember the exact words of his question. "Little girl, do you want to get an ice cream cone?"

I had paid attention in the safety assembly. I knew the answer to that one. "NO!" I shouted, and turned to run. But I had to make it past his car. (How long had he been watching me walk home with my schoolmates? Did he know my cul-de-sac was the last stop on the route and I walked two blocks further than my companions?) He started to cut me off, but at that moment a car rolled past, and in a flash the man was gone. When I think about that day, which is often, I realize that the unknown driver of that neighborhood car almost certainly saved me from one of the worst imaginable fates.

So by the time I had lived a decade in the world, I already sensed that public duty had failed and perverted desire reigned. Although my understanding of politics and culture is much different now than it was then, I still believe that much to be true. We live in an age of appetites.

Thus far we have examined the divided soul primarily from psychological, literary, and spiritual perspectives, but the implications also include the public realms. Socrates' famous maxim, "the city is like the soul,"[1] applies to duty and desire. Unquestionably the division of our age is skewed toward desire. When national governments fund gender assignment surgeries and companies sport slogans like "Just Do It," "Have It Your Way," and "Betcha Can't Eat Just One," we recognize that we are a desire-saturated society, obsessed with the fulfillment of our appetites and inclinations: material, sexual, or otherwise. The tyranny of desire has degraded the bonds of duty in every sphere of our humanity—individual, societal, and spiritual. No longer do we pledge allegiance to any code or standard higher than the individual self. We are ashamed of nothing and want everything, but desire cannot stand alone as a plumb line for human civilization. Without the mitigating balm of duty, the reign of desire unleashes chaos.

Much has been made of the so-called Culture Wars, but that is not a term I like. We are not fighting *against* culture but *for* it. What we need is a mending. No political or social construct is the culprit. As twentieth-century Soviet dissident Alexander Solzhenitsyn wrote:

> *The line separating good and evil passes not through states, nor between classes, nor between political parties either—*

---

1. Plato, *Republic*, 368d–369a.

> but right through every human heart—and through all human hearts. This line shifts. Inside us, it oscillates with the years. And even within hearts overwhelmed by evil, one small bridgehead of good is retained.[2]

From his eight years as a prisoner in the Soviet gulag, Solzhenitsyn understood that both the harm and the healing of the divided soul of our age begins not within its political structures, but within its people. For most of us the recovery of meaningful principles in the social sphere will manifest as a series of small works that take place in our homes, our workplaces, our communities, our families, and ourselves. Christ tells us, "The kingdom of God is within you,"[3] which means that the work of restoring public duty is personal.

One particular virtue, which is a potent antidote for the diseases of disordered desire that plague us, is fidelity. The union of duty and desire was ruptured by an act of faithlessness, thus it can be healed, at least in part, by keeping faith. Fidelity is a workaday virtue. It has dirty hands and wears work boots, and it looks like what Eugene Peterson calls, "a long obedience in the same direction."[4] I have noticed three important patterns or forms of fidelity to recover in our ordinary lives—particular love, the keeping of sacraments and vows, and repentance and forgiveness.

That term—"forms of fidelity"—is not just poetic alliteration, but practical actuality. A *form* is a shape or model of

---

2. Solzhenitsyn, *The Gulag Archipelago: 1918–1956*, 168.
3. Luke 17:21 (KJV)
4. Peterson, *A Long Obedience in the Same Direction: Discipleship in an Instant Society*.

something. An arch is an architectural form that upholds cathedrals. A muffin pan is a form that provides structure to baked goods. A sonnet is a poetic form that dictates the rhythm, rhyme, and meter of a poem. We rely on forms to make almost everything, and since fidelity is a virtue that requires action, it requires form. Just as we cannot stack blocks at random if we want to build an arch, neither can we be faithful to our duties without forms of faithfulness.

The first form of fidelity is particular love. This may be a clunky term, but in a cultural moment driven by ideology, it is vital to distinguish between meaningful love and its inverted and insubstantial shadow—abstract idealism. Christ calls us to love our neighbors, and He provides real-life neighbors in our daily lives—specific, particular human beings. We are too prone to put people in categories, judging by our own beliefs whether or not they are worthy of the dignity and care of love. But that is not love at all. The Scriptures tell us exactly what love looks like.

> Love is patient and kind; love does not envy or boast; it is not arrogant or rude. It does not insist on its own way; it is not irritable or resentful; it does not rejoice at wrongdoing, but rejoices with the truth. Love bears all things, believes all things, hopes all things, endures all things. Love never ends.[5]

This is the ethic at the heart of Victor Hugo's 1862 novel, *Les Misérables*, in which every central character is saved through particular love. When I say saved, I do not mean in

---

5. 1 Corinthians 13:4-8 (ESV).

the conventional sense of either saved from death or converted to Christianity, although both of those things happen in the story. I mean saved in a broader sense—changed, transformed, made new.

Les Misérables takes place in the tumultuous political climate of mid-nineteenth-century France, several decades after the French Revolution. Violence and poverty abound. The hero, Jean Valjean, has been imprisoned unjustly for stealing bread to feed his sister and her dying child. After nineteen years he is released, but nobody will hire a former convict until eventually the kind-hearted Bishop Myriel welcomes him off the streets. But Valjean resorts to theft once again, sneaking away in the night with the bishop's valuable silver. When he is caught, Bishop Myriel assures the *gendarmes* that he actually gave the silver candlesticks to Valjean. The Bishop tells the astonished Valjean that with the candlesticks he has purchased his soul for God and urges him to be an honest man. This Jean Valjean takes to heart, and everything good that happens next comes directly from Bishop Myriel's merciful act of particular love.

Jean Valjean learns his lesson well, and he dedicates himself to atoning for his former crimes. Within six years he becomes a benevolent factory owner and the mayor of his town, calling himself Monsieur Madeleine. During this season Jean Valjean helps many people—Fantine, Fauchelevent, Champmathieu, Cosette. Everybody he helps has a name and a life; everybody is a singular and particular person.

But not everybody is like Jean Valjean. *Les Miserables* presents two opposing extremes to particular love: reactionary self-righteousness in the form of the Inspector Javert and utopian idealism in the form of the revolutionary zealot Enjolras.

Inspector Javert correctly identifies that the moral fabric of France is unravelling in the wake of revolution, and he dedicates himself to enforcing the law. But in contrast to Valjean, Inspector Javert loves absolutely nobody. His only allegiance is to the letter of the law, weaponizing his civil authority against rule-breakers with neither pity nor mercy. He discovers that Jean Valjean jumped bail and dedicates himself to hunting Valjean down and imprisoning him forever. His obsessive pursuit represents the darkest version of distorted duty, when law seeks to annihilate love. His hatred extends so far that when Jean Valjean shows him mercy, he commits suicide. He would rather die than love.

Fleeing Javert, Jean Valjean moves to Paris with his adopted daughter, Cosette, now a young woman. The year is 1832, and Paris is torn by another impending revolution. A young revolutionary named Enjolras rallies a coterie of fervent youths to fight for liberty, equality, and fraternity. But the novel is not about the turmoil in Paris—it's about the people who suffer because of it. One idealistic young aristocrat named Marius joins the revolutionary cause, but love interrupts activism when he meets Valjean's adopted daughter, Cosette. The musical adaptation of the novel highlights this inner conflict when Enjolras chides him.

Marius, you're no longer a child
I do not doubt you mean it well
But now there is a higher call.

Who cares about your lonely soul?
We strive toward a larger goal
Our little lives don't count at all.[6]

Today, Enjolas' sincere but diabolical belief thrives in our own world, but the Christian gospel announces that Jesus Christ *does* care about our lonely souls. In the flesh He died a particular, human death so that we could live a particular, human life with particular ties to particular people and places. Christianity is not a social cause that justifies destruction in the name of duty, but a path of service motivated by love. Because of his blossoming love for Cosette, Marius leaves the revolution. His self-transcending desire for Cosette redefines his duty from an abstract cause to a particular person. And when he later returns to the barricade, it is less to fight in the revolution than to stand with his friends. Love for Cosette unites duty and desire in Marius' divided soul.

But another young woman, Eponine, is also in love with Marius. Eponine has been raised by thieves and hustlers. All she knows is poverty and violence, but her love ennobles her to ultimate sacrifice. On the eve of revolution, the mood in Paris is dangerous, and Jean Valjean flees the city with Cosette. Dejected, Marius returns to the barricade to rejoin the revolution. When a fatal shot rings out, Eponine leaps in front of the bullet, sacrificing herself to save Marius. Eponine dies a good death, laying down her life for the one she loved.

---

6. Claude-Michel Schönberg and Herbert Kretzmer, *Les Misérables: The Complete Symphonic Recording*, track 11, "Red and Black."

When Jean Valjean discovers Marius' whereabouts, he sets out to rescue his daughter's suitor, but by the time he arrives, the battle is lost. The revolutionaries are dead, along with their utopian vision. Jean Valjean combs through the wreckage to find the wounded Marius and carries him on his back through the Paris sewers to bring him home. He saves him for Cosette's sake—not because the boy fought bravely for a noble cause, but because he wants Cosette to be happy. Marius is saved through love, not idealism.

This complex web of interconnected relationships conveys that law and idealism ultimately fail, but sacrificial love for another—a particular other—brings healing to ourselves and our communities. From the moment that Bishop Myriel offers the silver candlesticks to Jean Valjean, *Les Miserables* is one long redemptive chain reaction propelled by particular love.

When we learn to love our neighbors, our bonds transcend the surrounding turmoil, cultivating a form of fidelity that harmonizes the confusion and conflict that threatens to disrupt our peace. But what keeps particular love from veering off course over time? The second form of fidelity that repairs the divided soul of a society is the keeping of sacraments and vows. One of the most grievous transgressions of modernity is the mockery and dismissal of promises. Oath-breaking strikes at the root of social order because it negates all trust and security.

A vow is a sacred and solemn promise. A sacrament, however, is something deeper. Historic Christianity understands sacraments like baptism, communion, and marriage to be physical manifestations of spiritual realities—forms of fidelity within the faith that impact our lives in very practical ways. For example, Christians believe that a fundamental transformation takes place when a couple is pronounced man and wife. Marriage is not a mere civil status, but the remaking of identities. A man and his bride were previously not married, but through the utterance of sacred words under sacred conditions, they become married. Something at the core of their beings shifts in the ceremony; a profound mystery is enacted. That *something*, that mysterious and fundamental shift, is the sacrament.

Let's turn again to Graham Greene's 1951 novel, *The End of the Affair*. Greene is a Catholic novelist who consciously explores the binding reality of sacraments and vows, choosing as his subject two sacraments, marriage and baptism, and, as you will recall, one vow made to God under duress. These forms of fidelity transform the course of the characters' lives in ways that are often unwelcome to them, but ultimately bring healing.

Sarah keeps her vow, and everything changes. Before the vow, she is married but faithless, and her faithless actions mirror her divided self. She is unhappy because her husband is insipid and her lover is cruelly jealous, but the actual betrayal of her marriage troubles her very little. But after her vow, Sarah becomes acutely aware of the incontrovertible fact that she is married, and that her married state is the obstacle to her desire for Maurice.

Sarah's vow to end the affair forces her to reckon with the actuality of marriage itself, placing its sacramentality at the center of her fragmented life. Because she is married, she must deny herself, break with her lover, and grapple with the existence of God. All of this is utterly new to her. Fidelity to her vow forces her to find a new way of being-in-the-world. She misses Maurice and resents Henry. This is painful, but it is evidence of the work of grace.

Soon a new crisis emerges. Sarah visits an atheist activist, hoping he will convince her once and for all that God does not exist. But instead she becomes increasingly worried that He does. As she struggles, she longs to reject God so she can be released from her vows. Her resistance conveys her dawning recognition that human fidelity is intrinsically connected to divine will, confronting her spiritual identity as well as her marital one.

At the proper time she finds God—quite literally. One night, lonely for Maurice and disconnected from Henry, she wanders into an empty church. Upon the wall hangs a lurid crucifix, and the body of Christ in all its wounded and bloody physicality is, for her, a mirror into the wounded and bloody sufferings of her divided self. By gazing at Christ's wounds, Sarah discovers her own, and she encounters grace.

Much later, after Sarah's death, something else comes to light. Her mother reveals to Henry and Maurice that Sarah was baptized when she was very young. So Sarah was a Catholic—lapsed, of course, and fragmented by her own doing, but always —even without her knowledge—a member of the sacramental communion of saints. The grace bestowed by baptism, the novel seems to claim, is irrevocable. By the end of her life, Sarah is reconciled to God, and her conversion catalyzes further transformation in the lives of those who loved her.

As Sarah shows us, keeping faith with sacraments and vows can be painful, but it is always healing. If we want to bring the balm of duty to the diseases of lopsided desire, we need to return to a culture of oath-keeping in our individual, communal, and spiritual lives.

But there is a third form of fidelity that heals the public breach between duty and desire—the active offering of repentance and forgiveness. Literary examples abound. This form of fidelity is so core to the human condition that virtually all stories converge toward some transformative moment of repentance and forgiveness. For my money, though, the best one of all is found in Homer's epic, the *Iliad*.

The *Iliad* opens in the tenth year of the Trojan war. The Greek armies are mustered at the gates of Troy to seize the faithless Helen from the arms of her Trojan lover, Paris, and return her to her husband, the Spartan king, Menelaus.

Many first-time readers of the *Iliad* are surprised to discover that the war is not the focus of the epic. Like *Les Miserables*, the *Iliad* is concerned with humanity far more than politics. In fact, the first line of the *Iliad* tells us what the story is really about: "Rage, goddess—sing the rage of Peleus' son Achilles."[7] The *Iliad* is not a story about the Trojan War. The war is merely the backdrop, the context, for something else—the rage of the warrior, Achilles.

The story opens when the god, Apollo, inflicts a plague on the Greek camp because King Agamemnon took a priest of Apollo's daughter as a warprize. When Achilles, the greatest warrior of the Greeks, publicly admonishes Agam-

---

7. Homer, The *Iliad*, 1.1.

emnon to return the girl to her father, Agamemnon angrily threatens to take Achilles' warprize, the beautiful Briseus, instead. This is a grievous insult to Achilles, an indefensible public attack on a noble warrior as well as the warrior code that defines them all. By doing this, Agamemnon violates fundamental tenets of Greek duty. Enraged by Agamemnon's betrayal, Achilles leaves the war, refusing to fight for his faithless general any longer. Agamemnon's unpardonable breach of duty is the catalyst for Achilles' rage.

By the final chapters, Achilles' rage has multiplied until he has alienated himself from his comrades and slaughtered hordes of soldiers. His dearest companion, Patroclus, is killed in battle by the Trojan prince, Hector. In retaliation, Achilles cuts Hector down in hand-to-hand combat, strings his corpse to his chariot, and drags his body around the Trojan walls in view of his family and subjects. Achilles has become inhuman, ravaged by grief and rage. But nothing assuages his wrath. No act of war can heal his desire for vengeance, soothe his longing for his friend, or restore his sense of duty as a warrior and citizen.

Day after day Achilles drags Hector's body around his friend's grave and weeps, but his tears bring no solace, no relief. "But Achilles kept on grieving for his friend, the memory burning on."[8] He neither eats nor sleeps, haunted by grief and longing.

The memories flooded over him, live tears flowing,
And now he'd lie on his side, now flat on his back
Now facedown again. At last he'd leap to his feet,

---

8. Homer, The *Iliad*, 24.4-5.

> *Wander in anguish, aimless along the surf, and dawn on dawn*
> *Flaming over the sea and shore would find him pacing.*
> *Then he'd yoke his racing team to the chariot-harness,*
> *Lash the corpse of Hector behind the car for dragging*
> *And haul him three times round the dead Patroclus' tomb,*
> *And he'd rest again in his tent and leave the body*
> *sprawled facedown in the dust.*[9]

But King Priam of Troy wants to bury his son. He knows that Achilles is still consumed with wrath. Priam, nevertheless, resolves to visit Achilles in the Greek camp in order to ask for Hector's body. When he arrives, he bows before Achilles, grasps his knees as a suppliant, and kisses his hands. The king tells Achilles that he had once been friends with Achilles' father. He speaks of his fifty sons, nearly all dead in the war, many of whom were killed by Achilles himself. And He ends his speech with these words:

> *Revere the gods, Achilles! Pity me in my own right,*
> *Remember your own father! I deserve more pity...*
> *I have endured what no man on earth has ever done before -*
> *I put to my lips the hands of the man who killed my son.*[10]

Stunned by Priam's humility and jolted beyond his own pain, Achilles responds.

> *These words stirred within Achilles a deep desire*
> *To grieve for his own father. Taking the old man's hand*

---

9. Homer, The *Iliad*, 24.12-21.
10. Homer, The *Iliad*, 24.12-21.

> *He gently moved him back. And overpowered by memory*
> *Both men gave way to grief. Priam wept freely*
> *For man-killing Hector, throbbing, crouching*
> *Before Achilles' feet as Achilles wept himself,*
> *Now for his father, now for Patroclus once again,*
> *And their sobbing rose and fell throughout the house.*[11]

Achilles lifts Priam from the ground and weeps again, but this time his tears are different. Now he weeps *with* Priam. This is the only time in the *Iliad* that Achilles does not weep alone. Priam's humility invites him into a healing experience of shared grief. Once irreconcilable enemies, they find each other in the borderlands of war trauma and forge a mutually restorative connection. Upon their shared lament, Achilles accepts Priam's ransom and returns the body of his son, agreeing to a twelve day truce so that both sides can mourn their dead. Priam takes Hector's body back to Troy to bury it in their community. And here the epic ends, not with the Trojan Horse or an arrow in the heel, but with the consolation of the rage of Achilles.

Through Priam's kiss, Achilles sees beyond his own rage and grief. Through Priam's humility, Achilles remembers his own father, reintegrating himself into family and community. His desire for vengeance and his longing for his friend is assuaged by seeing past his own misery into the sufferings of another, which in turn reorients him to his duties as a warrior, a Greek, and a prince. Priam's love for his dead son motivates him to gamble everything, to throw

---

11. Homer, The *Iliad*, 24.592-599.

himself at Achilles' mercy, which has been essentially non-existent until this moment. Priam humbles himself at the feet of the man who killed his son, deigning even to kiss his hands. This catalyzes a proper season of restoration not only between two individuals, but between nations as Achilles agrees to prevent the Greeks from attacking the city for the twelve days of Hector's burial honors. The final line of the *Iliad* is, "And so the Trojans buried Hector breaker of horses."[12] As they bury Hector, so they bury the rage of Achilles.

Humble repentance and forgiveness brings our disintegrated selves back into unity. Without them, we become monsters, bent inward toward our own pain. We see this everywhere. From the pervasive combat trauma of brutal international conflicts to spiteful hostilities on social media platforms, we are cruel to one another—and we excuse it. The sins of our society are many, and the backdrop of our public life is conflicted, but too many of us are prone to batter our enemies with ferocious accusation and abuse. Rage, however justified, will only deepen the divisions of this divided age. The Agamemnons of our time strike at the root of moral and civic order, but we have something the Greeks did not have: Christ's commandment to love our enemies and to pray for those who persecute us.

No doubt it is now obvious that I have been cheating. Only one thing is needed. All of the virtues that bring sanity and humanity into public culture rely on the fundamental Christian ethic, "love your neighbor as yourself."[13]

---

12. Homer, The *Iliad*, 24.941.
13. Mark 12:31 (ESV).

All forms of fidelity flow from this One Thing. I see much reactionary fear against the tyranny of desire, but it fails to help. Instead, the needful thing is to keep faith with the law of charity. We cannot heal the divided soul of our age by becoming divided ourselves. Restoring the bonds of duty in our divided age is a good and essential work, but for most of us, it will be a small one, made up of steadfast and intentional deeds like cooking family meals, filing our taxes, going to church, reading good books, voting our principles, keeping our promises, and repaying our debts. When I consider my role as a citizen, I expect the most influential work I will do is to walk steadfastly in what St. Thérèse of Lisieux called the "Little Way,"[14] doing ordinary things with extraordinary love.

---

14. Thérèse of Lisieux, *Story of a Soul: The Autobiography of St. Thérèse of Lisieux*, 207–210.

11

THE TRUE MYTH

Restoring the Broken Images

*"For me, reason is the natural organ of truth,
but imagination is the organ of meaning.*
— C.S. Lewis

Once, when I was three or four years old, I fell into a lake. My father was a seminary student and my mother a nurse, and they organized their schedules such that one of them was always with me, but it happened one day that my father needed to take a final exam that overlapped with my mother's day shift, so he brought me along. All of that is fact. What happens next lurks in the realm of myth.

In my memory my father leaves me at the verdant shores of a vast lake before disappearing behind the oaken doors of a stately mansion that I remember being much like Netherfield from the BBC's *Pride and Prejudice* miniseries. I am clad from head to toe in white raiment—a belted satin gown, white patent leather shoes, and ankle socks trimmed with lace. My hair is curled into soft ringlets. The lake is ringed with cattails casting dappled shadows on the water, blowing gently in the Oregon breeze. For a long time I gaze across the peaceful waters and daydream, but presently I notice a waterlogged stick floating near the shore. It seems like a nice stick, and it occurs to me that such a stick is likely to buoy a young adventuress across the smooth surface of a lake. Not being a lunatic, I consider this scientifically and come to the sage understanding that if a stick is already able to float, it will just keep on floating when passengers alight upon it. I decide to leap onto the stick so that the propulsion of my body would carry me *and* the stick gracefully across the expanse of the lake. I do not remember anything after the feeling of the stick giving way under my feet.

My father does not recall this event like I do, but he reports that once or twice I played outside the windows of his Systematic Theology classroom in plain view of his watchful eye and, when pressed, he remembers that, yes, one time I took a tumble into a shallow rainwater puddle and plastered myself with mud. I never owned a satin gown and nobody ever curled my hair.

Besides provoking much shared hilarity, none of my father's prosaic replies impact my memory of that day in the least. I *remember* the pattern of the lace on my imaginary dress and the allure of the sparkling waters of that fairytale lake. For some reason I told myself a story that became part of the inner lore of my psyche. What is so significant about that particular memory among the many thousands of forgotten moments of early childhood? I have often wondered. But this is part of the enigma that is the development of selfhood. The human instinct to define our lives by the stories we tell ourselves is universal. Our identities are story-formed on every level—psychological, social, and spiritual—and once a story implants itself, it requires a colossal effort to uproot.

This has important implications for the healing of our divided souls. As we have seen, we all bear the division between duty and desire within ourselves and manifest it in the world around us. In this way we are all little worlds, microcosms of the cosmic story, mirroring in ourselves the creation, fall, and restoration of all things. This is both universal and particular, meaning that the story of my life is in an archetypal and spiritual sense much like everybody else's, but the particular circumstances are wholly my own. For instance, you probably have not fallen into a lake-that-was-really-a-puddle, but chances are you hold a core memory that did not happen exactly as you recall. That is not a bad thing in itself; it is simply a clue that alerts us to the dissonance between perception and reality, between the stories we tell ourselves and the Story that transcends them.

The problem, however, is that when confronted with that dissonance, we are too prone to cling to human perception rather than divine reality. This is understandable, because we rightly rely on our perceptions to conceptualize reality, which is how our minds were created. In an undivided world, the confluence between perception and reality would be a vibrant source of intimacy between us as perceivers and God as reality, but the fall disrupted our communion with God and divided us not only from Him, but from our own selves. The result is spiritual blindness, "having the understanding darkened, being alienated from the life of God through the ignorance that is in them, because of the blindness of their heart."[1] This blindness prevents us from

---

1. Ephesians 4:18 (KJV).

perceiving the world as it actually is, rendering us vulnerable to dangers and temptations. And this pervasive spiritual blindness hinders us from recognizing and addressing the particular manifestations of disordered duty and desire in our divided souls. Disorder thrives in darkness, which makes curing our blindness necessary in order to restore the union between duty and desire.

Many of the perils and pitfalls of our spiritual blindness are avoidable. In this chapter, we will turn our attention to correcting our spiritual vision in order to heal our divided souls. To that end, I will speak in more general terms about the divided soul in the following pages, saying less about the specific nature of duty and desire and more about how to address the breach between them. This is not an abstract endeavor that takes place only in the mind, but a practical one that instantiates itself in the real world. We can't help that we are divided, but we can do something about it, which begins with subordinating our flawed perceptions to divine reality.

I told you the essentially trivial story of how I fell into a puddle, but most of us tell ourselves internal stories with much more at stake. So do I. For instance, I have suffered from insomnia for most of my life, but it became debilitating when my children were small. When I tucked them into bed at night, I became aware for the first time of the terror of human solitude. The fragility of their tiny bodies in the immense darkness took my breath away. I invented all sorts of menaces in the witching hours of the night—kidnappers, black widows, sleepwalking, SIDS. As the years passed the anxieties remained but morphed into different fears—driving, dating, friendships, family conflicts, faith, my own failures. I told myself the story that I was the only one standing between my children and catastrophe. For me this was the adult version of an old story I had absorbed in childhood—that my mother's sadness and rage were my fault, that I should protect everybody but myself from pain, that security is only possible by means of vigilance, that everything I love is always teetering on the edge of the abyss. These do not sound like stories; they sound like propositions, but they were lived as stories in episodes of chaos and despondency. And so when I laid my babies down in the darkness, I was afraid, and I knew exactly what Lewis meant when he wrote, "no one ever told me that grief felt so like fear."[2]

But here's the thing—I was wrong. My mother's suffering was neither my fault nor my responsibility. Her well-being was a burden far too heavy for my little shoulders to bear, and I buckled under it. Much of the sin and suffering I have carried throughout my life can be traced back to the fractures formed in my soul from those early experiences, but I did not have eyes to see that for a long time. I was blind. Blindness in itself is not a sin, but it is a disability that is exacerbated by the divisions within our souls. Disordered duty and desire obscure our spiritual vision from perceiving divine reality. That is what happened to me. What I did not know at the time was that God was carrying my mother and I, just as He is now carrying my children. Much pain would have been avoided if I had recognized that earlier. And it was not a series of theological arguments that opened my eyes to this, but a better, truer story.

---

2. Lewis, *A Grief Observed*, 1.

The term *story* encompasses many kinds of narratives—memories and myths, fact and fiction. Stories form our understanding of ourselves and our world, and they have the capacity to harm or to heal our divided souls in direct proportion to how they reflect the transcendent narrative of reality. The divided soul in ourselves and our world cannot be healed until we reconnect every story—psychological, social, and spiritual—back to the Christian story. Lewis articulates this in a letter to his friend Arthur Greeves.

> *Now the story of Christ is simply a true myth: a myth working on us in the same way as the others, but with this tremendous difference that it really happened: and one must be content to accept it in the same way, remembering that it is God's myth where the others are men's myths: i.e. the Pagan stories are God expressing Himself through the minds of poets, using such images as He found there, while Christianity is God expressing Himself through what we call 'real things.'*[3]

What Lewis called the True Myth is the story we return to again and again in these pages—the creation, fall, and restoration of the world through Christ. All stories are subordinate to this one. The True Myth is the healing story. As we have seen, our identities are intrinsically tied to the stories we tell ourselves. With this in mind, it becomes clear that personal and public narratives serve a fundamentally meaning-making function. To the private individual, this is

---

3. Lewis, *They Stand Together: The Letters of C. S. Lewis to Arthur Greeves (1914–1963)*, 191.

the realm of psychology and spirituality. But in the public square, it is a matter of myth. Myths are stories that shape everything. They form the framework of reason and imagination within societies and individuals, expressing eternal truths through narratives and images and holding enormous normative power for individuals and cultures.

The True Myth is the eternal reality that corrects the flawed perceptions of our divided souls. Throughout this book I have tried to habituate within myself and my readers a constant attention to the presence of the True Myth in every story, whether fact or fiction. The Beatitudes tell us that it is the pure in heart who will see God, which means that our perception of God's eternal presence is dependent on the cleansing of the inner eye of the soul. This requires prayerful attention and humble action. It seems to me that this can happen in one of two ways: either we eschew the world entirely and immerse ourselves in a wholly religious environment (as monastics do) or we take seriously Christ's words that "unto the pure all things are pure,"[4] and cultivate a spiritual vision that discerns everything within the framework of the True Myth. This is a path all of us can walk. Of course we know this transformation will not be complete until we enter the Kingdom of God, but until then we strive for wholeness.

But more often than not we simply do not recognize our flawed perceptions, believing that our choices and beliefs are founded on reasonable interpretations of true experiences and external standards of truth. But this is naive

---

4. Titus 1:15 (KJV).

and not only on the psychological level. Our flawed perceptions extend into the public domain as well. For example, modern materialists who value industrialized domination will approach a forest very differently than the ancient pagans who believed that tree spirits dwell within roots and branches. According to the materialist, trees are natural resources to be exploited, but to the pagan they are sacred vessels to be protected. Both responses are completely rational based on their story-formed assumptions about the nature of the world, but they are irreconcilable with one another.

This attention to first principles is why C.S. Lewis tells us in *The Voyage of the Dawn Treader* that Eustace Clarence Scrubb "read none of the right books,"[5] having his impoverished imagination malnourished only by "books of information" with "pictures of grain elevators" and "fat foreign children doing exercises in model schools."[6] The fact that Eustace's education was ludicrously lopsided does not mean that it was rational or scientific, but deficient, leaving him divided and diminished. And the only way for Eustace to be healed is through a living encounter with the reality of the True Myth. To that end Eustace is literally plunged into reality when he and his cousins plummet into Narnian waters through a forgotten painting of a stormy sea that his "up-to-date and advanced"[7] mother relegated to a back room. The analogy is profound—Eustace is forced to reckon with the real presence of a world beyond his vacant

---

5. Lewis, *The Voyage of the Dawn Treader*, 84.
6. Lewis, *The Voyage of the Dawn Treader*, 3.
7. Ibid.

imagination through the portal of a mythic image.

The cousins are taken aboard the Dawn Treader and included in a grand adventure. The others are jubilant, but for Eustace it is for a long time a terrible ordeal. At first he hates Narnia because he has no framework to understand it, no category for its living reality. His imagination has been, thus far, truncated and compartmentalized, kept hermetically sealed from the possibility of encroaching transcendence. Even in Narnia he tries to cling to an illusion of superiority, complaining about the Dawn Treader while "boasting about liners and motorboats and aeroplanes and submarines ('As if he knew anything about them,' muttered Edmund)."[8] He copes by writing vitriolic diary entries and demanding to speak to the British consul.

Nevertheless the adventure begins to work on him. When the Dawn Treader is damaged in a storm, the crew anchors near a wooded island to repair the mast. Eustace wanders off. He discovers a cave filled with treasure and, greedy for riches, falls asleep on a dragon's hoard. Since Eustace "had read none of the right books," he does not recognize the dangers of the dragon's lair, nor does he know that dragon gold is enchanted. While he sleeps, the enchantment takes hold, turning him into a dragon. "Sleeping on a dragon's hoard with greedy, dragonish thoughts, he become[s] a dragon himself."[9]

Eustace's transformation from boy to dragon springs from the ancient magic of Narnia, which is always meaningful, though often severe. Eustace's dragon-body is an

---

8. Lewis, *The Voyage of the Dawn Treader*, 28.
9. Lewis, *The Voyage of the Dawn Treader*, 91.

external manifestation of his internal greed, pride, and isolation. His predicament forces him to confront his divided soul, and "he realize[s] that he [is] a monster cut off from the whole human race."[10] This realization marks a fundamental alteration in Eustace's perception of himself, and his horde of petty grievances, complaints, and accusations fall away in an instance. "He beg[ins] to see that the others had not really been fiends at all. He beg[ins] to wonder if he himself had been such a nice person as he had always supposed."[11] Eustace responds to this painful recognition with repentance. "When he [thinks] of this the poor dragon that had been Eustace lift[s] up its voice and we[eps]."[12] In becoming a dragon, Eustace finally sees himself as he is, and his apparent malady is actually the cure for his spiritual blindness.

All of this is healing to Eustace's divided soul, but what happens now? Eustace is still a dragon, albeit a repentant one, and the Dawn Treader cannot remain anchored off the shores of a lonely island forever. What is to be done? Eustace is, well, perfectly useless in the matter of his own salvation. The only thing that can save Eustace is an intervening grace, an interruption of the grave justice that turned him into a dragon. And so one night Aslan visits Eustace, as we know he will. He leads him to a well of clear, clean water and tells him to undress. Remembering that dragons are "snaky sort of things"[13] that can shed their skin,

---

10. Lewis, *The Voyage of the Dawn Treader*, 92.
11. Ibid.
12. Ibid.
13. Lewis, *The Voyage of the Dawn Treader*, 107.

Eustace digs in his claws and scrapes off his dragon hide, but alas—all he does is reveal another layer of dry scales. Three times he attempts to peel off his skin before Aslan intervenes. "You will have to let me undress you."[14] The Lion sinks his claws so deeply into Eustace's dragon-body that he feels as if Aslan is tearing out his heart. But soon the scaly hide lies in the grass beside the pool, and the Lion immerses Eustace in the cleansing waters, and he emerges a boy again. This is, of course, Eustace's true conversion, when he is baptized into a new and truly human life.

Eustace's salvation begins with a violent collision between his divided soul and the reality of the True Myth. When he first arrives in Narnia the place is too difficult for his limited mind to accept, and he refuses to engage either in the duties required of a sailor or the desirable delights of the adventures on the Dawn Treader. Sometimes first encounters with divine reality are disorienting while entrenched perceptions try to assert dominance over new experiences. Somebody once told me that whenever we try to get free, there's always someone chasing us down, trying to reshackle us in our former chains.

Eustace is not alone in facing a transformative moment of healing self-recognition. In these pages we have met many characters like him: Mark Studdock, Rodion Raskolnikov, Gollum, Jane Eyre, Anna Karenina, and more. Each of these characters come face-to-face with their own frailty and make an irrevocable choice, whether for good or evil. Such crucial turning points don't just exist for the sake of dramatic tension; they ring true because they reflect the

---

14. Lewis, *The Voyage of the Dawn Treader*, 108.

True Myth. Eustace and others like him represent souls facing conversion who must die to their former selves in order to live as new creations.

Every time we see this in action, the True Myth roots itself a little bit deeper within us, one story at a time. This often takes place wholly unconsciously, especially when we are young. As Lewis says to Arthur Reeves, the story of Christ is a myth "working on us" as other myths do, planting within our minds an iconography of divine reality that illuminates the perceptive faculty of the soul. I have always said to my children and students that my only vocation as their teacher is to so populate their minds with iconic stories that if they ever try to flee from them, they will trip over the clutter on their way out the door. This is what happened to me. In my college years, I came close to despair, and I remember thinking how comforting it would if I were not a Christian anymore. I wondered if walking away from the faith would lift the burden of my conscience from my weary shoulders, but ultimately I could not do it because I knew, I knew, that the story of Christ was true. I saw it reflected everywhere, from Homer to Hemingway, the stories of divided souls undergoing trials and temptations, always dying in order to live, either literally or metaphorically. I recognized the pattern of divine reality, the fundamental meaning-making narrative of the True Myth woven throughout every story, including my own. There is no escaping the presence of the True Myth, nor the co-suffering Savior whose story it tells, and it began to occur to me that perhaps I, too, could be one of those rescued souls.

This is one of the reasons Lewis always claimed that he

came to Christ through the pagan stories and also why it is so important to read the right kind of books. If Eustace had internalized the True Myth earlier, he might have become happy and good long before entering Narnia. But Eustace grew up in the barren landscape of modernity. In his famous poem, "The Waste-Land," twentieth-century poet, T.S. Eliot, laments that the young, like Eustace, "know only a heap of broken images."[15]

Few of us would question that modernity has become a kind of spiritual wasteland, exchanging a fruitful life for a productive marketplace. And since the city is like the soul, we recognize that we often carry within ourselves an interior wasteland—a barren, starved inner geography of the soul, undernourished on broken images rather than the meaningful icons of goodness, truth, and beauty we crave. This is what happened to Eustace, who was before his conversion a "puny little person"[16] not by nature, but by education. He grew up in the waste-land, and his inner world was as dead and lifeless as his books about grain elevators and model schools. The essential point is that Eustace never read imaginative or ennobling stories, but only broken images—facts and information presented to him outside of a cohesive understanding of their intrinsic meaning.

All of this raises important questions about catechesis and education. In the 5th century BC, Socrates carried on a conversation with a man named Meno, who asked him whether virtue can be taught. Socrates convinces Meno that it can, but subverts his own arguments at the last minute,

---

15. Eliot, *The Waste Land*, line 22.
16. Lewis, *The Voyage of the Dawn Treader*, 4.

concluding the dialogue with the declaration that when all is said and done, virtue is a gift from the gods. We often ask the same question about salvation. Can it be taught, bequeathed, passed on? The theological tangles of such questions are beyond the scope of this book, but it seems to me that Socrates was onto something by equivocating. He argues at first that virtue must be a kind of knowledge, and since knowledge can be taught, so can virtue. The same argument can be applied to religious faith, and many parents and teachers seem to live as if it were so. But I disagree. I think virtue, like faith, cannot be taught. It must be acquired. A saint whose name I have forgotten once said that theology is not something we learn, but something we suffer, and in that way it is, as Socrates said of virtue, a divine gift. Once again, we need the True Myth, not to implement a rigid strategy of religious education, but to provide consolation and guidance to our depleted and divided souls, starving in the wasteland.

This is an important point, because I am about to advocate for the kind of books Eustace ought to have read long before his adventures in Narnia. However, I do not believe these books will save anybody. The best that they can do is reflect the story of Christ, but that is not all that they can do, nor all that they *should* do. If the only purpose of literature is to reflect the True Myth, we should give it up altogether because we already have the True Myth. Why keep the knock off if we have the real thing? But literature is not really a spiritual project; it's an earthy one. We write and read literature for the sake of the life we live here-and-now, which makes the literary tradition a collected iconography of the divided soul. All of this I have said before, but I return to it again because I believe the True Myth and the literary tradition work in tandem to correct our spiritual blindness, the first to draw our eyes to heaven and the second to rightly perceive the world.

All knowledge and culture coheres under Christ's authority, which gives us the freedom—and the responsibility—to preserve and pass on the world's intellectual and literary heritage. Christians ought to be the most exuberantly curious and intellectually hospitable people on the face of the earth, enriching our lives with the works of Homer, Shakespeare, the Brothers Grimm, Austen, Brontë, Dostoevsky, MacDonald, Tolkien, and more. The rich tradition of historic art and culture will most certainly not save us (only Christ can do that), but we can save it, preserving literature as a vital connection to the life of the world. By God's mercy, this does much to restore the harmony between human perception and divine reality, which enables us to see ourselves and God more clearly for the healing of our divided souls. Once we see the divisions between duty and desire within us, we can begin to take action, which is the subject of the next chapter.

Our identities are intrinsically tied to the stories we tell ourselves. Like Eustace, we become what we behold—a melancholy little girl reading *Anne of Green Gables*, Rochester calling for Jane across the moors, Raskolnikov kissing the earth at the crossroads, Sam bearing Frodo in his arms up Mount Doom, Prince Hal declaring his identity, Christ emerging from the empty tomb. Some of these stories are fiction, some fact, but all are meaning-making stories, illuminated by the True Myth, that can revive the waste-land around and within us.

12

THE DIVINE PHYSICIAN

How Christ Heals the Divided Soul

We have arrived at the final chapter having developed a kind of vision through which to perceive the mysteries of the divided soul. This vision is crucial, but perception is not enough. What can we do about it? I began asking this question very urgently as a college student, although I did not articulate it in the terms I employ today. But even then I understood that in certain calamitous ways I was not whole. In the normal course of things, however, I got married, became a therapist, had a child, and took a job at a local church. And at twenty-eight my fragile internal trusses collapsed. Looking back, I realize that the whole affair was sheer grace, but at first I was too frail to perceive it. What happened was that I got fired from my position at the church because I lied to my boss, who was also my mentor and my friend. The lie I told was small and senseless, which made it all the more grotesque. Earlier that week I had forgotten to complete a simple administrative task, and when asked, I panicked and lied. The woman (I will call her Deborah) was discerning, and she suspected my falsehood, offering me a chance to confess, but by then I was frightened and instead of humbly acknowledging my fault, I doubled down and lied again. The next morning, terrified of getting caught, I snuck into the office to cover up my mistake. It didn't work. Soon Deborah unearthed the whole story, and within days I was dismissed and publicly exposed—a letter went out to hundreds of families in the congregation explaining that I had been released from my position for committing "a moral failure of a non-sexual nature."

I was undone. My whole life I have been afraid of failing, because at the core of my being lurks a cringing certainty that mistakes disqualify me from love. In this case I created what I feared, and my shame was abject and absolute. But underneath the excruciating ignominy I felt, something transformative was stirring. My conscience acknowledged that what I had done was very wrong, that a grievous violation of true duty ought not to be excused or overlooked, and that this crucible of humiliation might yet be transfigured into true humility if I embraced repentance and love. My divided soul was laid bare, and the healing I needed was more than psychological—it was spiritual.

We must not fail to see that at the root of our psychological and social divisions is a spiritual catastrophe, a universal collapse of identity and cohesion following our first parents' renunciation of divine order. I hope it is obvious that a spiritual malady presupposes a spiritual remedy. Psychological, sociological, intellectual, and moral solutions fall short; the wound is spiritual, and so is its cure. Thus if we want to heal our divided souls we must look beyond conventional therapies and address the root spiritual cause. The early church fathers understood this, speaking of Jesus Christ as the "all-sufficient Physician of humanity"[1] and the church as "a hospital, and not a courtroom, for souls."[2]

Imagine, then, that you consult a specialist for a severe and chronic cough. The diagnosis is what you feared—lung cancer—and you are not surprised, because in this imaginary scenario you know of certain ominous risk factors in yourself, perhaps a family history of the same genetically-linked cancer and a habit of smoking a pack of cigarettes a day. Your family history is an inheritance over which you have no control, while smoking is an addiction formed by your own choices, and both likely contribute to your disease. When the doctor delivers your diagnosis, you are stricken to the heart. You cry out, "Forgive me!" But the doctor replies, "Forgive you? I am not your judge, I am your physician. I am not here to condemn you, but to save you." He recommends a course of treatment—surgery, medications, and healthy lifestyle changes. At this point you are each responsible for the different elements of your recovery; he offers a personalized healing plan for you to accept or reject. He prescribes the remedies; you take them. The surgery to excise the invasive disease is something only he can do, but taking your medicine and changing your life is up to you.

So it is with our diseased souls. Jesus Christ is the Divine Physician and we come to him plagued with soul-sickness. What is more, we are never absolutely sure of the sources

---

1. Clement of Alexandria, *The Instructor* (Paedagogus), 1.4.
2. John Chrysostom, *Homilies on the Gospel of Matthew*, Homily 50.

of our debased condition, whether in any given scenario we are inheriting or inflicting our self-destruction. More often than not it all mingles together. Either way, the cure is the same.

First, the Divine Physician interrupts the progress of the disease with a radical intervention—His incarnation, death, and resurrection. This is the surgical operation of grace. "I will give you a new heart, and a new spirit I will put within you. And I will remove the heart of stone from your flesh and give you a heart of flesh."[3]

Next, He utilizes His knowledge and skill to prescribe ongoing medicines, which are the shared healing practices of the church, including: prayer, fasting, study, confession, forgiveness, service, repentance, celebration, almsgiving. At this point the physician's expertise provides direction toward healing, but the rest requires our cooperation. If we do not act on his advice, these prescribed remedies, however efficacious, will produce no benefit.

The same is true for the final and most individualized prescription—the specific lifestyle changes necessary for each of us to cleanse and restore spiritual health. Depending on the gravity of our sins, we take more or less drastic measures, from deleting the internet browser on our phones to undertaking a vow of silence. We find relief from our vices in proportion to our efforts, as wholesome habits purify our bodies and minds. "Go and sin no more,"[4] says Christ to the woman caught in adultery, demonstrating that spiritual growth is a practical endeavor as well as a spiritual

---

3. Ezekiel 36:26 (KJV).
4. John 8:11 (KJV).

.one. Healing, then, is the result of divine help and human participation.

But what does this mean for us as we consider how to heal the divided soul? For me this is not an academic or intellectual query, but an existential one, all tangled up in the triumphs and failures of my own very ordinary, but nonetheless vivid and meaningful, life. I want a unified soul, but how? Only one Person can provide a trustworthy answer, and that is Christ the Divine Physician, "in whom all things hold together."[5] And since Christ is the true healer of our divided souls, we will turn to His teachings to identify unifying threads with which to stitch our fractured souls together.

In the parable of the sower, Christ points out the interior obstacles that keep us from thriving.

> *And he spake many things unto them in parables, saying, Behold, a sower went forth to sow; And when he sowed, some seeds fell by the wayside, and the fowls came and devoured them up: Some fell upon stony places, where they had not much earth: and forthwith they sprung up, because they had no deepness of earth: And when the sun was up, they were scorched; and because they had no root, they withered away. And some fell among thorns; and the thorns sprung up, and choked them: But others fell into good ground, and brought forth fruit, some a hundredfold, some sixtyfold, some thirtyfold.*[6]

Later in the same passage Jesus interprets the parable

---

5. Colossians 1:17 (ESV).
6. Matthew 13:3-8 (KJV).

Himself, telling his disciples that the seed is the "word of the kingdom," and the devil is the devouring birds. The soil, then, is the receptivity of the human heart to the gospel. The first type of soil is a hard heart where demonic resistance reigns. This heart is grievously divided, and the gospel message is snatched away. The second heart is "stony," or cluttered and superficial, lacking "deepness of earth." Such a person, having no "root in himself," welcomes the gospel as he welcomes any other trend from vegetarianism to small-batch beer, but his resolve collapses when he encounters resistance or difficulty. The shallow roots cannot support sufficient growth for bearing fruit. In this slothful soul neither duty nor desire are robust enough to anchor the gospel seedling in the inner life. The third type of soil seems more promising, at least at first, because the seed of the gospel germinates and tendrils begin to sprout. But alas, the message of the gospel "fell among thorns" which throttles the life out of the tender plants. Jesus tells us that the thorns are "the cares of this world" (disordered duty) and "the deceitfulness of riches" (worldly desires). These thorny temptations interrupt the progression of growth necessary for healthy flourishing.

But the story does not end with the stranglehold of thorns. Sometimes the seed of the gospel falls onto "good ground" and bears much fruit. Jesus freely communicates how to cultivate the conditions of the heart that promote thriving spiritual growth, conveying the unity of duty and desire inherent in the pursuit of a healthy soul. More often than not, His teachings are variations on the theme of temporal obedience (duty) in service of eternal delight (desire).

In short, Christ teaches us that all dutiful action is for the pursuit of joy. Consider, for instance, the Beatitudes from the Sermon on the Mount.

> *Blessed are the poor in spirit, for theirs is the kingdom of heaven.*
> *Blessed are those who mourn, for they shall be comforted.*
> *Blessed are the meek, for they shall inherit the earth.*
> *Blessed are those who hunger and thirst after righteousness, for they shall be satisfied.*
> *Blessed are the merciful, for they shall obtain mercy.*
> *Blessed are the pure in heart, for they shall see God.*
> *Blessed are the peacemakers, for they shall be called children of God.*
> *Blessed are those who suffer persecution for righteousness' sake, for theirs is the kingdom of heaven.*[7]

Meekness, endurance, purity, peacemaking—these are words of duty, but they are bookended by promises of happiness. Even the very grammar of Christ's precepts embeds duty within a framework of desire. The meaning of these characteristic teachings is that moral principles are not ends in themselves but serve an ultimate purpose, which is blessedness—a term that unites goodness with happiness, duty with desire. Achieving the blessed life, although not easy, is simple: "If you love me, keep my commandments."[8] Jesus Christ is the proper object of desire and keeping his commandments is the proper fulfillment of duty, and the latter springs from the former. Our humble obedience to

---

7. Matthew 5:2–12 (KJV).
8. John 14:15 (NKJV).

Christ is an essential ingredient of human participation that works alongside His intervening grace to repair every aspect of our fractured humanity. This means that if we want to heal our divided souls, we must do everything to love Christ and keep His commandments.

Of course this raises the question: what are the commandments?—a question Jesus answers many times in the gospels with the ancient words of the Torah,

> Then one of them, which was a lawyer, asked Him a question, tempting Him, and saying, "Master, which is the great commandment in the law?" Jesus said unto him, "Thou shalt love the Lord thy God with all of thy heart, soul, mind, and strength. This is the first and great commandment. And the second is like unto it. Thou shalt love thy neighbor as thyself. On these two commandments hang all the law and the prophets."[9]

Once again, then, we arrive at the supremacy of love, which heals the divided soul because it is in itself the perfect intersection of duty and desire. Contrary to a common misunderstanding of Christ's teachings, law is not contrary to love; rather, "love is the fulfilling of the law," (Romans 13:10). The love of God heals us insofar as we offer it back in the forms of worship ("love the Lord thy God") and charity ("love thy neighbor as thyself"). To the extent that we love God and our neighbor, we fulfill all duty and purify all desire. As I said, this may be simple, but it is not easy. In the short-term, the cost is high. "If any man wants to come

---

9. Matthew 22:35-40 (KJV).

after Me, let him deny Himself, take up his cross daily, and follow Me."[10] The world, the flesh, and the devil haunt the dissonance between *ought* and *want*, spawning chaos and calamity. The Prodigal in us wants to squander our Father's inheritance on wild living, while the internal Older Brother keeps toiling joylessly in the fields. But Christ invites us to take a side against the temptations of the fallen world and ally ourselves with Him instead. In the parable of the talents, Jesus urges us to serve Him in *all* things, even the aspects of our lives that do not on first blush appear overtly "spiritual."

> *For the kingdom of heaven is as a man travelling into a far country, who called his own servants, and delivered unto them his goods. And unto one he gave five talents, to another two, and to another one; to every man according to his several ability; and straightway took his journey.*
> *Then he that had received the five talents went and traded with the same, and made them other five talents.*
>
> *And likewise he that had received two, he also gained another two.*
>
> *But he that had received one went and dug in the earth, and hid his lord's money.*
>
> *After a long time the lord of those servants cometh, and reckoned with them. And so he that had received five talents came and brought other five talents, saying, "Lord, thou*

---

10. Luke 9:23 (ESV).

delivered unto me five talents: behold, I have gained beside them five talents more."

His lord said unto him, "Well done, thou good and faithful servant: thou hast been faithful over a few things, I will make thee ruler over many things: enter thou into the joy of thy lord."

He also that had received two talents came and said, "Lord, thou delivered unto me two talents: behold, I have gained two other talents beside them."

His lord said unto him, "Well done, good and faithful servant; thou hast been faithful over a few things, I will make thee ruler over many things: enter thou into the joy of thy lord."

Then he which had received the one talent came and said, "Lord, I knew thee that thou art an hard man, reaping where thou hast not sown, and gathering where thou hast not strawed: And I was afraid, and went and hid thy talent in the earth: lo, there thou hast that is thine."

His lord answered and said unto him, "Thou wicked and slothful servant, thou knewest that I reap where I sowed not, and gather where I have not strawed: Thou ought therefore to have put my money to the exchangers, and then at my coming I should have received mine own with usury. Take therefore the talent from him, and give it unto him which hath ten talents. For unto every one that hath shall be given, and he shall have abundance: but from him that hath not shall be taken away even that which he hath. And cast ye the unprofitable servant into outer darkness, where there shall be weeping and gnashing of teeth."[11]

The New Testament term *talent* ("talanton") does not refer to aptitude or ability, but to an ancient measurement of weight, commonly used to apportion standard amounts of currencies like gold and silver. In this case the man who goes on a journey entrusts his servants with substantial funds that should be invested to enrich his estate. But the parable also encompasses the more common English use of the word *talent*, specifying that the Master divvies out the money in proportion to each servant's "several ability." The servants' duty is to put their talents (in both senses of the word) to work increasing the Master's fortunes, but ultimately neither the seed money nor the return on investment belongs to them. At the proper time they submit the fruit of their labors to their lord for his blessing. They dedicate everything to their vocation—time, energy, competence, creativity—subordinating their own wills to the will of their lord. To the "good and faithful servants," duty is devotion (a word that certainly implies desire), manifesting in a lifetime of voluntary service.

But the "wicked and slothful" servant makes no effort at all. He buries his talent underground, failing even to deposit the funds in a bank where it can accrue interest. When called upon for a reckoning, the Slothful Servant blames his Master for his own laziness, deflecting respon-

---

11. Matthew 25:14-24 (KJV).

sibility and accusing his lord of cruelty and injustice. This servant is "wicked" because he violates his master's trust and attempts to cover it up; he is "slothful" because he fails to complete the good work entrusted to him.

The parable of the talents offers a unified earthly vision of duty and desire, inviting us to imitate the Faithful Servants by obeying Christ in everything. Serving God like this is not at all the same thing as living like the Older Brother, and a primary difference is in the expectation of reward. The Older Brother and the Faithful Servants are similar in their diligence and accomplishments, but dissimilar in their motivations. As you remember, the Older Brother spurns the Father's invitation to come to the feast, preferring to nurse his grievances rather than celebrate his Prodigal brother's return. In spite of his endless toil in the fields, the Older Brother is actually more like the wicked and slothful servant, blaming the Father for his own failures and resisting joyful communion with his neighbors. Ultimately, God allows his lazy sons and servants to reap what they sow, whether the Older Brother to his self-imposed exile from the table or the "unprofitable" servant to "outer darkness, where there shall be weeping and gnashing of teeth." These divided souls choose to remain sick and wounded because they will not abide in the healing hope of heaven.

But the Faithful Servants know better. They work just as hard as the Older Brother, and they welcome the master's blessing when it comes. The work itself is good, but it is the humble heart that transfigures it into joy. On many occasions St. Paul calls us "the bondservants of Christ," equating us to Faithful Servants whose temporal vocations exist to achieve an eternal reward. My own occupations include writing, research, teaching, parenting, and more. Yours are something else. They are all meaningful because they are the lives we are given, and our faithfulness and service matters, and all of it "worketh for us an exceeding and eternal weight of glory."[12] It befits us to work humbly and thoroughly, not as the Older Brother and the Slothful Servant who eschew their rewards to cosset their complaints, but as a sort of virtuous hedonist who desires to be made worthy of blessedness. "And whatsoever ye do, do it heartily, as for the Lord and not for men, knowing that of the Lord ye shall receive the reward of your inheritance."[13]

But I run the risk of communicating that life is mere drudgery in exchange for heaven. Certainly that is not totally false, and we cannot claim any measure of comfort and ease as our due. One of the great mysteries of life on earth is the inequality of pleasure and pain among its inhabitants. Allowing that temporal happiness is elusive, does that mean it is unattainable? And if happiness is attainable, then to what extent and how do we attain it? Many times in His ministry Jesus warns us against the pursuit of worldly and fleshly pleasures. One such warning is found in the parable of the Rich Fool.

> *And he spake a parable unto them, saying, "The ground of a certain rich man brought forth plentifully: And he thought within himself, saying, 'What shall I do, because I have no room where to bestow my fruits'? And he said, 'This will I*

---

12. 2 Corinthians 4:17 (KJV).
13. Colossians 3:23-24 (KJV).

do: I will pull down my barns, and build greater; and there will I bestow all my fruits and my goods. And I will say to my soul, Soul, thou hast much goods laid up for many years; take thine ease, eat, drink, and be merry.'

But God said unto him, "Thou fool, this night thy soul shall be required of thee: then whose shall those things be, which thou hast provided. So is he that layeth up treasure for himself, and is not rich toward God." And he said unto his disciples, "Therefore I say unto you, Take no thought for your life, what ye shall eat; neither for the body, what ye shall put on...But rather seek ye the kingdom of God; and all these things shall be added unto you."[14]

Jesus Christ is utterly clear that every one of us must make a final choice between two competing priorities— the kingdom of God and the kingdom of this world. If we choose the first, we will also gain the second, but if we choose the world, both kingdoms will slip from our grasp. "No man can serve two masters: for either he will hate the one, and love the other; or else he will hold to the one, and despise the other. Ye cannot serve God and mammon."[15] But does this mean that Christians must renounce all pleasures as polluted mammon? Surely not, since the Psalmist prays, "thou wilt shew me the path of life: in thy presence is fullness of joy; at thy right hand there are pleasures for evermore."[16] In this verse joy and pleasure are interchange-

---

14. Luke 12:16-22, 31 (KJV).
15. Matthew 6:24 (KJV).
16. Psalm 16:11 (KJV).

able, which indeed they would be if duty had not been severed from desire. Pleasure is not the enemy of the soul. In fact, St. Paul reminds us that "whether...the world, or life, or death, or things present, or things to come; all are yours. And ye are Christ's; and Christ is God's."[17] In the proper order of things, Christians enjoy the good things of life, because the only thing denied to us in the whole universe is sin. Literally everything else, writes the Apostle Paul, is ours.

The problem with the Rich Fool in the parable is not that "his ground...brought forth plentifully," but that he "is not rich toward God." The man is a fool because his good fortune fed his vices rather than nourishing his virtues. He is a divided soul who failed to enjoy the agricultural bounties of the natural world as real pleasure, choosing instead to exploit them for his own selfish gain. The problem, then, is not pleasure itself, but the sins that corrupt it, as C.S. Lewis explores in *The Screwtape Letters*.

Screwtape is an epistolary novel that explores the subtle art of temptation through an imaginary correspondence between a Senior Tempter named Screwtape and his young protegee, Wormwood. With Screwtape's guidance, Wormwood's job is to lure a nameless human "subject" away from God, and he nearly succeeds. But in Letter 13 we learn that Wormwood has sustained a "defeat of the first order"[18] when his subject experiences a renewal of grace. Screwtape castigates Wormwood for his failures as a Tempter. His crime, according to Screwtape, is allowing the young man

---

17. 1 Corinthians 3:22-23 (KJV).
18. Lewis, *The Screwtape Letters*, 63.

to experience "two positive Pleasures."[19] The first is reading a book "he really enjoyed,"[20] and the second was taking a long walk in country, which "he really likes."[21] According to Screwtape, these are fatal blunders because real pleasure prevents demonic access to human personhood.

> *How can you have failed to see that a real pleasure is the last thing you ought to have let him meet? Didn't you foresee that it would just kill by contrast all the trumpery which you have been so laboriously teaching him to value? And that the sort of pleasure which the book and the walk gave him was the most dangerous of all? That it would peel off from his sensibility the kind of crust you have been forming on it, and make him feel that he was coming home, recovering himself?*[22]

Wholesome pleasures are potent medicines for mending the divided soul. The demons work hard to corrupt pleasure not because it is wicked, but because it is *good*. If the Rich Fool had allowed himself *real* pleasure in the fruitfulness of his lands, his good fortune would have been no rival to God and he might have welcomed heaven the night his soul was required of him. Authentic pleasures armor us against temptation because when we develop a taste for goodness, we do not crave vice, and the humble pleasures of earth become for us harbingers of eternal joys. What's more, they also serve as remembered tokens from Eden.

---

19. Lewis, *The Screwtape Letters*, 64.
20. Ibid.
21. Ibid.
22. Ibid.

When we enjoy good things without guile and for their own sake, we recover something of the innocence and freshness of that lost paradise, and such humble delight is a kind of happy return to our true selves as we were meant to be.

Real and therefore healing pleasures must be wholesome in themselves and enjoyed for their own sakes. Probably they will be quite ordinary activities like hiking or woodworking or growing vegetables—far humbler than heaven, but nonetheless pure. They will be neither destructive nor wasteful nor ugly, disqualifying many foolish and wicked habits that drain our time and energy, like scrolling on our devices or getting drunk. Screwtape tells Wormwood that he would go very far to prevent us from cultivating simple pleasures because there is "a sort of innocence and humility and self-forgetfulness about them"[23] that inoculates the human soul against the assaults of the world, the flesh, and the devil. Of course pleasures must take a proper place in our lives (nobody can spend all their time bird watching or playing piano sonatas), but that is where we come full circle and remember that if we love God and our neighbors, we will fulfill the whole law and experience the freedom to enjoy a good life. As I have already said, these pleasures are not owed to us, but we can receive them freely when they come because they are good medicine for the soul.

Pleasure is, of course, the opposite of pain, but both render us vulnerable to temptation. We are perilously susceptible to falling into sin through both, but Jesus Christ teaches us exactly what to do when we discover fractures of division within us—and that is to repent. The command to "Repent,

---

23. Lewis, *The Screwtape Letters*, 66.

for the kingdom of God is at hand!"[24] is the first mandate in all four gospels, and the New Testament connects repentance with salvation over fifty times. In the Greek, the word for repentance is metanoia, which literally means "change of mind." Repentance is not a single action but a permanent posture of humility and obedience. For most of us, the mind-shift of repentance will be slow and habitual, a steadfast submission of the self to God over time. When we truly repent, we remember our sins without despair and we cast ourselves upon God's mercy. Our example is Mary, the Mother of our Lord, who was "greatly troubled" when the angel praised her virtue, and who responded to the Annunciation with, "Behold, I am the handmaiden of the Lord. May it be to me according to your word."[25] Repentance, then, is the needle and divine love is the golden thread that closes the wounds of our divided souls. Truly love covers a multitude of sins, and once again we encounter the mysterious interweaving of God's mercy and human participation.

These remedies are not human inventions, but divine aid, and they are ours for the taking. All of them continue to mend my own divided soul which I faced so starkly all those years ago when I was dismissed from my job at the church. Even then I was no stranger to suffering and shame, but that public disgrace was my first honest encounter with my own naked unworthiness. What I remember most about it is a deep awareness of myself as a wounded sinner along with an ardent longing to be made whole again. Neither feeling has left me since. And soon after it all happened, I

---

24. Matthew 3:2 (KJV).
25. Luke 1:29, 38 (KJV).

read this passage in the Old Testament book of Lamentations.

> *It is good for a man that he bear the yoke in his youth.*
> *He sitteth alone and keepeth silence, because he hath borne it upon him.*
> *He putteth his mouth in the dust; if so be there may be hope.*
> *He giveth his cheek to him that smiteth him: he is filled full with reproach.*
> *For the Lord will not cast off for ever.*
> *But though he cause grief, yet will he have compassion according to the multitude of his mercies.*
> *For he doth not afflict willingly nor grieve the children of men.*[26]

It came over me then that everything that had ever happened in my life was part of a vast cosmic collusion for my salvation—my complicated childhood, my tattered copy of *Anne of Green Gables*, my brave but fragile mother, my tragic college romance, the auburn-haired stranger on a motorcycle, my hemorrhaged babies, even that shameful moral failure of a non-sexual nature. Glory to God for all, all things. In that transfiguring moment I gave thanks to God that He loves me enough to chastise me, and I prayed for His will to be done. Behold, I am the handmaiden of the Lord. May it be to me according to His word.

Since then I have read Wendell Berry's magnificent novel, *Jayber Crow*, which conveys the hard-fought reality of spiritual transformation.

---

26. Lamentations 3:27-33 (KJV).

> But now I was unsure what it would be proper to pray for, or how to pray for it. After you have said 'thy will be done,' what more can be said? And where do you find the strength to pray 'thy will be done' after you see what it means?[27]

I know that I am not alone—we are most assuredly all divided souls, but the hands of the Divine Physician stitch us back together. May God have mercy on us and remember us in His kingdom—and may we, as Faithful Servants, someday receive the longed-for blessing: "Well done, thou good and faithful servant: thou hast been faithful over a few things, I will make thee ruler over many things: enter thou into the joy of thy lord."[28]

---

27. Berry, *Jayber Crow* (Washington, D.C.: Counterpoint, 2000), 51.
28. Matthew 25:21 (KJV).

ACKNOWLEDGMENTS

My whole life I have always wanted to read books, write books, and talk about books. Only the first of these is enjoyable to do alone, so I am grateful for the efforts of a host of people who make the others achievable. Glory to God for all things. The first fruits of my gratitude go to David Kern, who essentially found me in obscurity and made me his friend and then, unbelievably, his colleague. Everybody stumbles upon some happy serendipity in life, and David is mine. Thank you for editing nearly everything I have ever written—and for all the other things. Not for nothing do we live like butter scraped over too much bread. Thank you to Graeme, who always orders two drinks at a time and, like Michelangelo, sees the angel in the marble and carves until he sets him free. Thank you to Encyclopedia Scan, who knows everything, loves the right things, and is able to locate page numbers for quotes at lightning speed if you are ever writing a book with a million citations. Thank you to my godfather, Andrew, for providing the insight that led to this book, for marrying my adored Karen, and for leading me out of the cave.

Thanks to Tim, Logan, and Melissa for making me sound better than I normally would. Thank you to my beloved family, Scott, Jack, and Lucy, who make it easy for me to unite duty with desire every day of my big, beautiful life. I love you madly. Thank you to Emily—after virtue, friendship. And finally, to the Close Reads Podcast community, thank you for talking about books with me, David, Tim, Sean, and each other.

"We have been invited into their lives, from which we will never be evicted, or evict ourselves."
—Wallace Stegner.

Bibliography

Aristotle, *Nicomachean Ethics*, trans. W. D. Ross, rev. J. O. Urmson, in *The Complete Works of Aristotle*, vol. 2, ed. Jonathan Barnes. Princeton: Princeton University Press, 19840.

Austen, Jane. *Sense and Sensibility*, ed. Ros Ballaster. London: Penguin Books, 2003.

Berry, Wendell. *Jayber Crow*. Washington, D.C.: Counterpoint, 2000.

Brontë, Charlotte. *Jane Eyre*. New York: Penguin Classics, 2006.

Chrysostom, John. *Homilies on the Gospel of Matthew*, Homily 50.

Clement of Alexandria, *The Instructor* (Paedagogus).

Dostoevsky, Fyodor *Crime and Punishment*, trans. Richard Pevear and Larissa Volokhonsky. New York: Vintage Classics, 1993.

Eliot, T. S. *The Waste Land*. New York: Boni and Liveright, 1922.

Euripides, *Hippolytus*, trans. David Kovacs. Cambridge, MA: Harvard University Press, 1995.

Greene, Graham. *The End of the Affair*. New York: Penguin Books, 1962.

Hass, Robert. *Praise*. New York: Ecco Press, 1979, "Meditation at Lagunitas."

Hicks, David V. *Norms & Nobility: A Treatise on Education*. Lanham, MD: University Press of America, 1999.

Homer, The *Odyssey*, trans. Robert Fagles. New York: Penguin Books, 1996.

Julian of Norwich, *The Revelation of Divine Love in Sixteen Showings Made to Dame Julian of Norwich*, trans. M.L. del Mastro. New York: Image Books, 1977.

Lewis, C.S. *That Hideous Strength*. New York: Scribner, 2003.

Lewis, C. S. *Perelandra*. New York: Scribner, 2003.

Lewis, C. S. *Perelandra*. New York, NY: Simon & Schuster, 2003.

Lewis, C. S. *The Weight of Glory and Other Addresses*. New York: HarperOne, 2001.

Lewis, C. S. *A Grief Observed*. San Francisco: HarperOne, 2001.

Lewis, C. S. *They Stand Together: The Letters of C. S. Lewis to Arthur Greeves (1914–1963)*, ed. Walter Hooper. New York: Macmillan, 1979.

Lewis, C. S. *The Voyage of the Dawn Treader*. New York: HarperCollins, 1980.

Lewis, C. S. *The Screwtape Letters*. New York: HarperOne, 2001.

Milton, John. *Paradise Lost*, ed. John Leonard. London: Penguin Books, 2000.

O'Connor, Flannery "The Fiction Writer and His Country," in *Mystery and Manners: Occasional Prose*, ed. Sally and Robert Fitzgerald. New York: Farrar, Straus and Giroux, 1969.

Peterson, Andrew. "All Things New," *Resurrection Letters, Volume II*, Centricity Music, 2008, track 4

Peterson, Eugene H. *A Long Obedience in the Same Direction: Discipleship in an Instant Society*. Downers Grove, IL: InterVarsity Press, 1980.

Rilke, Rainer Maria. "Autumn," trans. Jessie Lamont, in *Poems*. New York: Tobias A. Wright, 1918.

Saint Porphyrios, *Wounded by Love: The Life and Wisdom of Saint Porphyrios*, trans. John Raffan. Limni Evia, Greece: Denise Harvey, 2005.

Schönberg Claude-Michel and Kretzmer, Herbert. *Les Misérables: The Complete Symphonic Recording*, directed by John Caird and Trevor Nunn. London: First Night Records, 1988, track 11, "Red and Black."

Shakespeare, William *Hamlet*, in *The Norton Shakespeare*, edited by Stephen Greenblatt et al. New York: W. W. Norton & Company, 1997.

Shakespeare, William. *The Merchant of Venice*, in *The Norton Shakespeare*, edited by Stephen Greenblatt et al. New York: W. W. Norton & Company, 1997.

Shakespeare, William. *Henry IV, Part 1*, in *The Norton Shakespeare*, ed. Stephen Greenblatt et al. New York: W. W. Norton & Company, 1997.

Shakespeare, William. *Much Ado About Nothing*, in *The Norton Shakespeare*, edited by Stephen Greenblatt et al. New York: W. W. Norton & Company, 1997.

Shaw, George Bernard. *Pygmalion*. London: Penguin Books, 2003.

Sidney, Sir Philip. *Astrophil and Stella*, "Sonnet 31," in *English Renaissance Poetry*, ed. John Williams (New York: Dover Publications, 1990).

Solzhenitsyn, Aleksandr. *The Gulag Archipelago: 1918–1956*, trans. Thomas P. Whitney. New York: Harper & Row, 1973.

Thérèse of Lisieux, *Story of a Soul: The Autobiography of St. Thérèse of Lisieux*, trans. John Clarke, OCD. Washington, DC: ICS Publications, 1996.

Thompson, Silouan. "Divine Eros According to Saint John Chrysostom," SilouanThompson.net, July 2024.

Tolkien, J.R.R. *The Fellowship of the Ring*. Boston: Houghton Mifflin, 2004.

Tolkien, J.R.R. *The Two Towers*. Boston: Houghton Mifflin, 2004.

Tolkien, J.R.R. *The Letters of J.R.R. Tolkien*, ed. Humphrey Carpenter. Boston: Houghton Mifflin, 1981, Letter 186.

Tolstoy, Leo *Anna Karenina*, trans. Richard Pevear and Larissa Volokhonsky. New York: Penguin Books, 2000.

Undset, Sigrid. *Kristin Lavransdatter: The Wreath*, trans. Tiina Nunnally. New York: Penguin Books, 1997.

Yeats, W. B. "The Crazed Moon," in *The Winding Stair and Other Poems*. London: Macmillan, 1933.

ABOUT THE AUTHOR

Heidi White, M.A., is a teacher, therapist, literary podcaster, and author with a lifetime of experience as a divided soul. She lives in Colorado Springs with her husband and children. You can follow her on Instagram @heidiwhitereads and on Substack @closereads.substack.com.

This book is set in Iowan Old Style, a typeface designed by John Downer and released by Bitstream in 1991. It is inspired by serif typefaces from Renaissance Italy, now called the "old-style" or Venetian model of typeface design.